Preaching Through the Bible

1, 2 Thessalonians

Michael Eaton

Sovereign World

Sovereign World
PO Box 777
Tonbridge
Kent, TN11 9XT
England

By the same author:
Ecclesiastes (Tyndale Commentary) – IVP
The Baptism with the Spirit – IVP
How To Live a Godly Life – Sovereign World
How To Enjoy God's Worldwide Church – Sovereign World
Living Under Grace (Romans 6–7) – Nelson Word
A Theology of Encouragement – Paternoster
Preaching Through the Bible (1 Samuel) – Sovereign World
Preaching Through the Bible (2 Samuel) – Sovereign World
Focus on the Bible: 1, 2, 3 John – Christian Focus

ISBN: 1 85240 180 X

Typeset by CRB Associates, Reepham, Norfolk
Printed in England by Clays Ltd, St Ives plc.

Preface

There is need of a series of biblical expositions which are especially appropriate for English-speaking preachers in the Third World. Such expositions need to be laid out in such a way that they will be useful to those who put their material to others in clear points. They need to avoid difficult vocabulary and advanced grammatical structures. They need to avoid European or North American illustrations. *Preaching Through the Bible* seeks to meet such a need. Although intended for an international audience, I have no doubt that the simplicity of the series will be of interest to many first-language speakers of English as well. This book is the first to present an exposition of some New Testament epistles.

These expositions will be based on the Hebrew and Greek texts but will take into account three translations of the Bible; the New King James (or Revised Authorised) Version, the New American Standard Version and the New International Version. The expositions will be comprehensible whichever of these versions is used, and no doubt with some others as well. In this exposition I have supplied my own translation.

It is not our purpose to deal with minute exegetical detail, although the commentator often has to do work of this nature as part of his preliminary preparation. But just as a good housewife likes to serve a good meal rather than display her pots and pans, so the good expositor is concerned with the 'good meal' of Scripture rather than the 'pots and pans' of dictionaries, disputed interpretations and the like. Only occasionally will such matters have to be discussed. Similarly matters of 'Introduction' do not receive detailed discussion. A simple outline of some introductory matters is found in the first chapter and an appendix makes some suggestions about further study.

Michael A. Eaton

Contents

Contents

Author's Preface

I have preached through 1 and 2 Thessalonians more times than I can remember! My most recent full exposition, wholly within one congregation, was in the Intensive Discipleship School of 'Chrisco Fellowship of Churches' a few years ago. More recently I have been preaching through the letters *huko na huko* ('hereabouts and thereabouts'), as they say in Swahili, in different parts of Kenya. Over the years I have given more attention to 1 Thessalonians than to 2 Thessalonians but recently have tried to correct the balance and have been preaching on both letters as I have been writing these chapters.

In my translations I try not to use too much male bias! And my ungrammatical 'everyone ... they', and similar oddities which appear occasionally, are an attempt to shape the English language so as to be more pleasant to half of the human race. But I do not call God 'She' and there are some non-sexist extremisms that I do not yet like. Maybe I'll get used to them later. But I am not fussy and the word 'he' maybe comes more than it ought.

To Jenny; to Tina Gysling, my daughter, who works through my material; to my son Calvin who helped me write chapter 9; to Chris Mungeam, and to other faithful friends in Jesus – many thanks.

Michael A. Eaton

Chapter 1

Introducing 1 and 2 Thessalonians

Paul was born in Tarsus and had once had a family home there (Acts 9:11). He spoke Hebrew or Aramaic as his home language and spoke Greek as a foreign language. He came from a fairly prosperous home, for he was sent to Jerusalem to be educated and his father was a Roman citizen. As a young man he hated anything to do with Jesus, but then about AD 34[1] he experienced a dramatic conversion, and God told him his life's work would be that of preaching to Gentiles.

About ten years after his conversion Paul was invited to join an older Christian preacher, Barnabas, in ministering to Gentiles in Antioch. He spent about a year there (AD 46–47) and became a well-established teacher of the gospel. It was from Antioch that Paul and Barnabas were sent out to reach Gentiles further afield. In AD 47 they went by boat to Cyprus and then to the north eastern coast of the Mediterranean sea, preaching and founding new churches. Then they came back to Antioch and reported what had happened. Their trip must have taken about a year (AD 47–48).

Some time later Paul felt they should go on a second ministry tour, starting with visits to the churches they had founded a year or so previously. Paul and Barnabas disagreed sharply about Mark, and so sharp was the disagreement that they divided the areas between them and Barnabas and Mark went to Cyprus while Paul and Silas

11

went round the coast. So the second ministry-tour of Paul began.

In the spring of AD 50 Paul and Silas went northwards up the Mediterranean coast encouraging the churches in Syria, then following the coast they turned east and continued through Cilicia still encouraging the churches along the way (Acts 15:41). They came to Derbe, then to Lystra (Acts 16:1) and it was at this point that Paul met Timothy and invited him to travel with them in ministry (Acts 16:2–3). They continued travelling eastwards, passing through Iconium (Acts 16:2) and then through the Phrygian and Galatian region, that is, through the south of the Roman province of Galatia (Acts 16:6). Finally they reached Troas (16:8), which was as far east as they could go, if they were to stay within that part of the mainland. It was a port on the Aegean Sea, and was further east than they had been on their previous journey.

They were not sure where to go next but that night God called them in a vision to cross the sea that was between Troas and Europe. Soon after, they left Troas by boat and landed at Samothrace on the other side (Acts 16:11). From there they travelled to Neapolis (Acts 16:11) and then reached Philippi (Acts 16:12). They stayed there 'some days' (Acts 16:12) during which many striking events took place (Acts 16:13–40). Then they travelled further going through Amphipollis and Apollonia and reaching Thessalonica (Acts 17:1). To begin with Paul went to the synagogue and for three weeks preached to Jews, having some success as he preached (Acts 17:2–4). But then opposition came and the Jewish authorities used drifters from the market-place to start a riot against Paul, Silas and Timothy. They had been staying with a sympathetic Jew named Jason and his house was invaded by the mob (17:5). Jason himself was physically assaulted and accused before the local magistrates of being a violent troublemaker (17:6–8). Jason was forced to ensure that Paul and Silas would leave the city. They were both forbidden to return (17:9) but Timothy was not affected by the magistrates decision (as 1 Thessalonians 3:1–5 makes clear).

Organised persecution obviously continued after Paul and Silas had left (see 1 Thessalonians 2:13–14; 3:3) but the church stood firm and became a centre of further outreach (1 Thessalonians 1:8). Judging from 1 Thessalonians 1:9, many Gentiles were saved at this time.

Paul went on to Beroea and Athens (Acts 17:10, 15). While in Athens he sent Silas and Timothy to Thessalonica to find out how the church was doing. By the time Timothy got back Paul had gone on to Corinth, where he stayed during the time from the autumn of AD 50 to the spring of AD 52. 1 Thessalonians was written from there probably about late AD 50. 2 Thessalonians was sent shortly after (perhaps early AD 51).

So it was Paul who pioneered the church in Thessalonica. His ministry there caused a tremendous upheaval in the local society, and soon there was much suffering for the church. Paul himself was criticized. Evangelistic successes always lead to attack from the devil; this may take the form of criticism, or extremism within the church. Nothing arouses the devil more than conversions.

Let us try to get a profile of this church. It will help us to see what a 'church' is meant to be.

1. **It was born amidst a burst of spiritual power**. It is obvious that Paul had great spiritual power when this church began. Paul began by preaching in the synagogue. His preaching raised violent opposition and disturbed the entire town (Acts 17:2–9). Why is it that we often seem to think that 'church-planting' takes a long time? Paul started this church in three weeks, yet the Thessalonians' conversion was dramatic and clear. They turned from idols to God and immediately began to live in the light of Jesus' second coming (1 Thessalonians 1:9–10).

2. **It was sustained by the Holy Spirit with very little leadership**. Paul preached in Thessalonica for a short time and then was forced to leave. One might think that the church would have little hope of survival, but actually it became vibrantly powerful and was much used by God in the surrounding areas. In 1 Thessalonians Paul is giving lots of instructions to young Christians about how to live. He is not there with

them personally but he is sending this inspired letter and trusting that his letter and the Holy Spirit will enable these young Christians to live a godly life. They have strong leadership (Paul) but he is not there personally. They have the Scriptures (Paul's letters). They have the Holy Spirit. When God is at work and Christians are alive with zeal and love, they can stand despite great opposition.

3. **It became a church throbbing with activity for God**. Paul speaks of its work and labour and persistence (1 Thessalonians 1:3). It was obvious to Paul that these Thessalonians had been chosen by God. What made him sure was the way in which the Spirit had obviously worked so powerfully (1 Thessalonians 1:4).

4. **It became a church which combined great joy with much suffering**. They received the Word with much affliction, says 1 Thessalonians 1:6, and one only has to read the story in Acts 17 to see what Paul meant. There was physical violence and false accusation while Paul was there and organised persecution after he left. There was evidently a slander campaign against Paul (for in 1 Thessalonians 2 Paul is defending himself against possible accusations).

5. **It became a model and an encouragement to other churches**. Although this church was a distinct congregation it apparently had contacts with churches throughout the province of Macedonia in which Thessalonica was to be found, and also had contacts further south in Achaia where Corinth was the most notable city. These other churches knew all about Thessalonica and received inspiration from the way they were rejoicing amidst trials.

6. **The congregation at Thessalonica could make mistakes**. We can see from Paul's letter that they were making mistakes concerning the second coming of Jesus. A congregation which is full of the Holy Spirit can still make mistakes. But this does not worry Paul. He sends his letter and expects that the Holy Spirit will restore the balance in Thessalonica.

7. **The congregation at Thessalonica became a centre of evangelism**. The Word of the Lord *'sounded forth'* from them. They apparently found ways to make sure that the surrounding areas heard about Jesus and soon the entire area had

heard about Jesus through what had happened to these Thessalonian Christians.

This is the profile of just one New Testament church. It had spiritual power, and soon became a church throbbing with activity for God. Most of this activity seems to have been connected with evangelism. The activities were not little tea-parties or comfortable talks on how to manage your garden or how to bring up your children to look nice and respectable! It was a persecuted church, sustained by the Holy Spirit and with very little leadership. Paul is concerned about godliness and spreading salvation to surrounding areas. This is what he expects 'church life' to be. The Word of the Lord is to be *'sounding forth'*. Yet the church had needs. There was a lot of excitement over the doctrine of the Second Coming. The Thessalonians began to think the Second Coming of Jesus would be within weeks or months. Some stopped working. They were very young Christians and needed guidance as to how to live.

So Paul wrote 1 Thessalonians. He wanted to share some thoughts about his ministry in Thessalonica in such a way as to answer criticisms and doubts. He wanted to encourage them amidst sufferings, to tell them more about the Second Coming of Jesus, and to help them with regard to Christian living.

We have a wonderful glimpse of what early Christians were like, not long after the outpouring of the Spirit at Pentecost. Here we see a glimpse of Christian preachers ministering in the power of the Spirit, and a church which is authentically a church alive with the life of God.

Footnote

[1] The dates of Paul's life are not totally certain. I speak dogmatically in the interests of brevity. My dating of the events in Paul's life is similar (but not identical) to that of F.F. Bruce.

Chapter 2

A Great Christian at Prayer
(1 Thessalonians 1:1–3)

Paul begins his letter by describing himself, addressing himself to his readers and giving his greeting (1:1). *'Paul and Silvanus and Timothy, to the church of the Thessalonians in God the Father and the Lord Jesus Christ. Grace to you and peace.'* (1:1).

Then, as generally in his letters, he starts to give thanks to God before he gets to the main concerns of his letter. 1 Thessalonians 1:2–5 is one long sentence in Paul's Greek. It begins: *'We thank God always concerning all of you...'* (1 Thessalonians 1:2a), and then is followed by three clauses:

'...making mention [of you] in our prayers unceasingly,
...remembering your work...labour...patience...
...knowing your election...'.

In English, it is better to put it into smaller sentences. It is a simple opening but it give us a glimpse into the world of the early Christians. Our interest is in four matters.

1. **Paul's description of himself**. The letter comes from *'Paul and Silvanus and Timothy...'* (1:1). He describes himself very simply, and he associates himself with his fellow workers. Although he is the writer of the letter he associates himself with others. Team-ministry of some kind is always necessary in the church of Jesus Christ. No minister can do everything himself. No preacher has all the gifts needed for the work of God. If any worker has good wisdom he will associate himself with a team of fellow-workers.

16

2. **Paul's references to God's grace and peace**. He gives his greeting. Normally a Greek letter simply said 'Greetings!' but Paul says something more spiritual than that! His greetings could be called 'half-prayers'. They are greetings but genuine desires for the people he writes to. His greatest longing for his friends is that they might know God's grace – God's help amidst every circumstance they are in. And he hopes that they will be at peace – enjoying such a sense of being reconciled with God that they can face anything.

3. **Paul's description of the church**. He describes it as the *'church of the Thessalonians in God the Father and the Lord Jesus Christ'* (1:1).

In giving his thanks to God for them, he tells us more. *'We give thanks to God always for all of you, making mention of you unceasingly[1] in our prayers* (1:2). *We remember your work of faith and your labour of love and the endurance that comes from your expectation concerning our Lord Jesus Christ, in the presence of our God and Father'* (1:3).

This church was a church 'in God'. It means that their existence as a church was supernatural. This church was not simply a club or a religious organisation. It was conscious of God as its source of energy, its guide, its protector.

This church was energetically serving God. Paul speaks of *'work ... labour ... endurance'*. Every church has a calling, just as every individual Christian has a calling. There are things that God will put before each congregation for it to do. Not that the church is a gang of slaves. This work arises in a special kind of way. It is not a drudgery. It is not like going to the office or to the factory. It is work and labour and persistency that comes from 'faith ... love ... expectation'. What happens is that God puts challenges before His people. It may be an opening to share the gospel. It may be a situation of great need. It may be that a local government office is in some kind of need and asks the local congregation to help. In one way or another God puts before the congregation an invitation to achieve something for Him. And the congregation responds in faith, in love, in the expectation that God is about to do something good.

This church was conscious of the presence of God. Any

congregation will become like a secular 'club' unless it is conscious of the leading and the presence of God. The Thessalonians were a people of faith and love and expectation because they were aware of *'the presence of our God and Father'*.

4. **Paul's reference to his praying**. Paul's prayer life is seen here in his passing references to prayer. **It included thanksgiving**. *'We give thanks to God...'*. It was **steady and constant and all-embracing**. Paul prayed *'...always for all of you ... unceasingly...'*. He liked to mention his praying. It was not that he wanted to boast about how much he prayed, but he wanted the people he was writing to, to feel that they were being prayed for. It is good to feel that someone is praying for you. And it is good to give encouragement to others by letting them know that you pray for them.

We shall discover that the church at Thessalonica was not a faultless church. There is no such thing as a 'faultless' church, even in the New Testament. People often talk about wanting to be like the 'New Testament churches'. What we mean is that we want to obey the New Testament scriptures as much as possible. Fine! But it ought to be remembered that not even the churches of the New Testament times were without weaknesses.

No, the church at Thessalonica was not 'faultless', but it was an excellent church nevertheless. A church which was 'in God' and had an apostolic leadership concerned about God's grace and God's peace. A church led by an apostle like Paul who was a man of prayer. A church which lived in the consciousness of 'the Lord Jesus Christ'. Such a congregation might not be faultless, but it was 'in God' and 'in Christ', and that is what matters. While God is leading it and they have the guidance of a man like Paul to steer them, they can expect that God will use them.

Footnotes

[1] 'Unceasingly' could belong to verse 3 (*'unceasingly calling to mind...'*) (see Bruce, *Thessalonians*, p. 10), but the three parallel clauses suggest it belongs with verse 2.

Chapter 3

Chosen to Salvation

(1 Thessalonians 1:4–7)

Paul is thanking God for the Thessalonians (*'We thank God...'*, says 1:2). At the same time he is helping them to get a good view of what happened to them when they came to faith in Jesus. When you come to experience Jesus' salvation you have to get a clear grasp of what has happened to you.

1. **Salvation is the result of God's predestination**. Paul says *'We know, brothers and sisters, beloved by God, that you have been chosen...'* (1:4). Behind our salvation and our coming to faith is the plan of God. *'As many as were ordained to eternal life believed'* (Acts 13:48).

For Paul, predestination to salvation is a fact! It may be mysterious and we must be careful about how we use this truth about ourselves. We must not become fatalists, but it is a fact that we believed in Jesus because God had chosen us even before our believing. All the praise for our salvation goes to Him. For Paul this is deeply reassuring. The Thessalonians are being persecuted. The knowledge that God chose them for salvation will greatly steady them amidst their troubles and conflicts.

2. **The evidence of our being chosen is our response to the gospel**. How did Paul know that God had chosen the Thessalonian Christians? Did he have some kind of access into the secret and hidden plans of God before the foundation of the world? No, we cannot **directly** know who are God's

chosen ones, and we should not approach the subject in this way. When we think about God's plans, we should always come at them **from behind**. What I mean is that it is possible to see the predestination of God **after the events** and not before. Paul did not go to Thessalonica asking about who was chosen by God! He simply preached to everyone and called upon everyone to believe in Jesus. But **after the event**, when many people wonderfully responded to Jesus, Paul knew that the hand of God was in what had happened. He says *'we know ... that you have been chosen* (1:4), *because our gospel did not come to you in word only but it came to you in power and in the Holy Spirit and with much conviction'* (1:5). What made Paul know that God had chosen these Thessalonians to salvation was the way in which they responded to the gospel. Don't try and investigate the plans of God ('What am I predestined to do?'). Instead respond to Jesus! After you have come to salvation, after you are walking in obedience you can give all the praise to God for what has happened. What happened in Thessalonica was that the people responded wonderfully to Paul's preaching. This is what made Paul know that God had chosen them to salvation.

3. **The heart and centre of what happened in the spiritual awakening at Thessalonica was a combination of the word of God and the Holy Spirit**.

Paul says *'our gospel did not come to you in word only but it came to you in power and in the Holy Spirit and with much conviction ... '* (1:5a).

The balance between 'Word and Spirit' is well-known, although it does not answer all questions (since most people think they are 'balanced'!).

In our preaching there has to be 'word'. There must be substance. Christian ministry is proclamation, a clear announcement of what God is doing. There is the telling of good news in a comprehensible manner. In the gospels Jesus would teach publicly in the synagogues, in the temple courts, or in the open air. There must be word. Our God has plenty to say.

Yet the power of the Holy Spirit must also be present.

How does this 'power of the Holy Spirit' show itself? It is not just 'phenomena'. Sometimes, when preaching is in the power of the Holy Spirit, there are unusual phenomena. There may be unusual effects on people's bodies. But this is not the main thing, and the apostles did not deliberately seek 'phenomena' although unusual events often took place as they preached.

This power of the Holy Spirit brings liberty of speech. It is clarity of understanding, authority, fearlessness. Think of Peter's preaching on the day of Pentecost. A few weeks before he had been muddled and confused, and had avoided being involved with Jesus at the time of Jesus' arrest. When the Spirit came upon him, he was immediately given what to say and said it with great liberty, fearlessness and a deep revelation of what had happened in the death and resurrection of Jesus. Within seconds he had a depth of understanding of what had just happened on the day of Pentecost.

This power of the Holy Spirit brings 'much assurance'. The preacher has assurance about what he is preaching. The people have a deep conviction that what they are hearing is from God.

4. **Both the preachers and the people became illustrations of the grace of God**. Paul can say: *'Similarly you know what sort of people we were when we were with you for your sake* (1:5b). *And you, on your part, became imitators of us and of the Lord, for you received the word, amidst affliction, with the joy of the Holy Spirit* (1:6). *And so you became an example to all the believers in Macedonia and Achaia'* (1:7).

Paul was well-known and the people were able to take him as a model of how to live the Christian life. But then they became examples of God's grace also. People began to look to them, just as they had looked to the apostle Paul and his friends. Paul was a model to them of godliness and steadfastness amidst persecution. Then they became good examples of godliness and steadfastness also. This is how the church of Jesus spread so rapidly. It was the combination of the word of God, powerful enabling by the Holy Spirit, and visible results in the lives of the people. It is this that makes the church what it is meant to be.

Chapter 4

Experiencing Salvation

(1 Thessalonians 1:8–10)

Paul goes on telling of how he is thanking God for the Thessalonians. His thanksgiving leads into a description of what happened when the gospel came to the Thessalonians. We can look at what happened when they believed, what were the results of their believing, and what was the content of what they believed in.

1. **What happened when they believed**. The preaching of Paul in that part of Greece was obviously powerful and influential. Paul says ... *you became an example ... For from you the word of the Lord has rung out. Not only in Macedonia and Achaia but in every place your faith in God has become known, so that we do not need to tell other people about you* (1:8). *For the people themselves report what sort of welcome we had among you ...* ' (1:9).

When the Holy Spirit is at work, the message of the gospel not only comes to the people, also the news 'rings out' in the surrounding communities. Paul's word here means to sound forth, to ring out noisily, to make a noise that everyone hears.

When people powerfully experience God's salvation they cannot keep quiet about what has happened. It bursts out of them. Everyone gets to see it. The news goes around the nearby communities.

This is the way in which the gospel of Jesus spreads around

the world. It is more powerful than books and films and advertising campaigns. It reaches people who do not have television and who never get to libraries. When we ourselves are gripped by what has happened to us, we simply cannot hold it back in quietness and timidity. The news of what happened in Thessalonica went to the surrounding areas quite spontaneously. People would want to tell their relatives and cousins what had happened to them. They would perhaps organise groups of people to spread the news to the nearby villages and towns. When Paul and his friends went to these towns the news about Thessalonica had already gone ahead. 'Yes, Paul', they would say, 'we have heard about you and your preaching already! We were told about what happened in Thessalonica . . . . ' Paul did not have to tell other people about the Thessalonians; other people told him. 'Yes, Paul, we know. Let me tell you about what happened to my cousin . . . . ' The people themselves reported what had happened.

2. **The immediate result of their believing**. Basically they came to *'faith in God'* (1:7) – that is faith in the God of the Bible, the God and Father of our Lord Jesus Christ.

But Paul describes in detail what this faith immediately led to in their personal lives. The story went around about the welcome the apostles had, *'and how you turned to God from idols to serve the living and true God* (1:9). *And they report how you are awaiting His Son from heaven, whom He raised from the dead, Jesus, who delivers us from the wrath which is coming'* (1:10).

By faith they turned away from idols. They saw their idols as useless and dead. When we are gripped by faith in the God and Father of our Lord Jesus it will give us the boldness and confidence to turn away from idols. It does not matter whether the idols are the demons and evil spirits of old-fashioned paganism, or the idols of power and money and worldly pleasures. Either way, only faith in God will enable us to break away from them.

By faith they turned to something as well as away from something. There was a turn-around in their lives when they believed the gospel and met the true and living God. They discovered God is genuine. They discovered that God is alive. They came to have a daily awareness of God. They would talk to Him. He would speak to them. They would pray to Him. He would answer their prayers. God is not just an idea, a theory in a book. God is alive!

By faith they started looking eagerly for God's Son, Jesus, to come again from heaven. It did not matter to them how long it would take for Jesus to come. They started living with their eyes fixed on the expectation of His coming.

3. **The content of what they believed in**. Their faith was not simply optimism or cheerfulness. It was not 'faith in faith'. The important thing about having faith is what you are having faith in. In the case of the Thessalonians their faith had content; it was definite faith in some basic facts about Jesus.

It was faith in Jesus' death on the cross. They knew that Jesus was raised *'from among dead people'* (1:10).

It was faith in Jesus' resurrection. They believed in *'His Son . . . whom He raised from the dead'*. They knew that Jesus was alive.

It was faith in Jesus' ascension. They knew that Jesus was not physically present on planet earth in the way He had once been physically walking around in the streets of Jerusalem and in the villages of Galilee. They knew He was now in heaven.

It was faith in Jesus' Second Coming. They were *'awaiting His Son from heaven . . . '*. They knew that Jesus would come again; visibly, sensationally, not as a baby but as king of the universe.

It was faith in Jesus' ministry to them personally. Their Saviour was, as they knew, *'Jesus, who delivers us from the wrath which is coming'*. The day of Jesus' coming will be a day of God's retribution. All evil will be exterminated. All debts and obligations will be paid. All quarrels will be settled. God's righteous anger against all wickedness will fall upon every manifestation of sin. But the Thessalonians had no fear. They knew that the one who had already saved them would rescue them in that day of retribution. When Jesus comes, the one who has already forgiven us, saved us, cleansed us, invigorated us with God's powerful Holy Spirit, will rescue us when the wrath of God finally comes.

Chapter 5

Faithful Ministry

(1 Thessalonians 2:1–4)

Paul is praising God for the wonderful things that happened when the Thessalonian church had come into being. But at the same time there is a purpose behind his reminiscences. He wants the Thessalonians to view Paul himself in the right way.

It is obvious that Paul was being greatly criticised and slandered in Thessalonica. The pagan friends of the Thessalonians were not happy with Paul. They regarded him as a disturber of the peace. The gospel always causes controversy. Anyone who is empowered by the Spirit to preach as Paul preached is going to cause something of a stir.

Paul's way of dealing with criticism is to write simply about what had happened at Thessalonica. This is a good way of handling criticism. You make sure none of the criticism is true. You are open and friendly. In these verses Paul can appeal to the Thessalonians' knowledge of him. They know all about him. He can simply appeal to their memories and their personal observation of what he was like (see 2:1, 2, 5, 9, 10, 11). Then he gives a simple description of the facts. It is a good way of handling criticism.

1. **He had not been ineffective; he had been full of boldness** (2:1–2). Paul wanted them to remember what great things had happened at Thessalonica. *'For you yourselves know, brothers and sisters, about our coming among you. You know that it was not in vain* (2:1), *but having previously suffered and*

having been insulted at Philippi, as you know, we had the bold-ness in our God to speak to you the gospel of God in the midst of much conflict' (2:2). Paul is able to point to the success of his ministry. He did not come *'in vain'*, and to no effect. The best evidence for the genuineness of the gospel is what it does in the lives of the people who receive it. Paul can say: 'you remember what happened. Our visit to you was powerfully effective in changing your lives, wasn't it? You remember, don't you?'

When Paul and his friends came to Thessalonica he had only just come from Philippi (see Acts 16:12–17:1). During that time at Philippi they had been imprisoned and beaten with wooden rods (Acts 16:22). They had been insulted. Though Paul was a Roman citizen and a highly educated man, he was arrested on a false charge, stripped of his clothes and treated as a criminal. You would think that at that point he might want to give up his career as a travelling preacher! But no. He went on to Thessalonica and started preaching there just as he had done at Philippi!

Despite his great sufferings Paul had been given the bold-ness of the Holy Spirit. *'We had boldness in our God...'*.

This is what Christian ministry is like. There is no promise of an easy life, but in the midst of what might happen to us, God's Holy Spirit will give us boldness.

2. **He had not been deceitful; he had a commission from God** (2:3–4a). Christians who declare the gospel boldly are likely to be viewed with suspicion. 'There is a trick some-where', people will say. 'What is in it for you? You are a deceiver with some clever plan....' Paul wants the Thes-salonians to understand him. *'For our exhortation does not come from error or from impurity, and it does not come with deceit* (2:3). *No, but as people who have been approved by God to be entrusted with the gospel, we speak, not to please other people but to please God who tests our hearts'* (2:4).

A Christian truly in the will of God knows that what he or she is saying is from God. The Christian is not a philosopher hoping that he might discover the truth and making all sorts of blunders along the way. God has revealed His gospel. *'Our exhortation does not come from error...'*.

Equally the Christian may know that the sources and the motives of his preaching are good and clean. It does not spring from any kind of wickedness or impurity. It does not come with guile or cleverness, like a man trying to sell something which is not worth having.

No, Paul and his friends have been approved by God. God is rewarding Paul for his genuineness and sincerity. Many times Paul has been tested, and he has been found faithful. When we prove ourselves faithful God trusts us with more. Paul had been found faithful and now God was trusting him with more.

3. **He had not been a man-pleaser; he lived to please God** (2:4b). The Christian is to be sensible about not offending people needlessly, and we are accountable to the wider church of Jesus Christ. Yet ultimately we are not living to please other people; we are living to please God.

It is wonderful to know that it is possible to please God. We know that we are simply forgiven sinners. Yet we are not to think that we are so sinful that we can never please God! On the contrary, this is one of the secrets of living a godly life. We live to please God. If we live this way, it will deliver us from hidden wickedness. We know that God is able to see what others cannot. It will deliver us from the fear of others. The unreasonable criticisms that come our way will not trouble us too much. Our eyes are on God. He is more searching than anyone else. He 'tests our hearts'. Yet He is more gracious, more loving, more tender than any human supervisor will ever be.

The secret of ministry is to be conscious of being called by God, trusted by God, watched by God, tested by God and loved by God. If we are men and women who are conscious of God in this way, we shall be able to endure amidst many trials. When criticised we search our hearts, we state the facts, we do what we can to avoid needless misunderstanding – and then we leave the rest to God.

Chapter 6

Sincerity in God's Work

(1 Thessalonians 2:5–8)

Paul is gently defending himself and his friends against criticism. He is putting into their hearts and minds a right way of thinking about themselves and of the ministry of the apostle Paul.

He has said that his ministry was characterised not by ineffectiveness but power (2:1–2), not by deceit but by a commission from God (2:3–4a). He had not lived as a man-pleaser but as one who pleases God (2:4b).

Now he makes the point that he was not self-seeking but self-sacrificial (2:5–8). He puts it negatively and positively, speaking of the behaviour they avoided (2:5–6) and of what their style of life was actually like (2:7–8).

Consider **the behaviour they avoided** (2:5–6). Paul says: *'For we never came with words of flattery, as you know. Nor did we come with a pretext for greed – God is witness (2:5). And we did not seek glory from people, either from you or from others, although we had the ability to impose ourselves on you with full weight, as apostles of Christ'* (2:6).

1. **It was without flattery**. 'Flattery' is when you talk to people insincerely, with the hope of using them, or getting them to support your own personal concerns. There was nothing like this in Paul's mind when he ministered the gospel of Jesus Christ.

2. **It was without greed**. There were many travelling teachers in the ancient world who wandered around the

29

world trying to use their gift of talk to raise funds for themselves. It has been a problem that has troubled the church of Jesus Christ as well. Perhaps in nations which despise the gospel, this is not a problem, but the more successful the preaching of the gospel is, the more there is a danger of precisely this style of 'ministry' gaining influence.

3. **It was without pride**. *'We did not seek glory from people, either from you or from others'*, says Paul. There are a number of false motivations that may spoil the work of God. It may be the desire for money, but equally it may be the desire to be someone important. Paul was not like that – and he gave proof of his disinterest in seeking glory by going to the hardest of pioneer situations, places *'where Christ was not named'* (Romans 15:20). Glory-seekers normally do the exact opposite. They go only to places where there are plenty of Christians already, and therefore plenty of generous supporters! Paul was simply not like that. He knew it and they knew it.

4. **It was without domination**. Although Paul was conscious that he could have used great authority, for the apostles were 'first' in authority (see 1 Corinthians 12:28; Ephesians 4:11), yet in fact he avoided heavy domination. (The word 'apostle' is used in at least six ways in the New Testament; here it seems to refer to pioneers sent out to plant churches.) They could have been very authoritative but they used as little authority as possible. Heavy authority may be needed at times (as Paul's other letters bear witness) but when they could, they preferred to be gentle.

Consider next **the behaviour they followed** (2:7–8). The letter continues: *'But we were gentle among you, like a mother tenderly caring for her own children (2:7). Having in this way a great affection for you, we were pleased to share with you not only the gospel of God, but also our very lives, because you had become very dear to us'* (2:8).

1. **It was with tenderness**. Paul's attitude towards the Thessalonians was that of *'a mother tenderly caring for her own children'*. Paul's words refer to a mother who breast-feeds her child and treats her baby with great gentleness. Paul likes to use many picture-words in referring to himself. He is a

herald, a father, a steward, and – in this place – a mother breast-feeding her baby.

2. **It was with affection**. Paul liked to speak of his affection and describe himself as *'having ... a great affection for you ... you had become very dear to us'*. He was not too shy or too proud to be an affectionate person. Although he had only recently got to know these Thessalonians he had taken them into his heart, and wanted them to know how much he loved them. They were foreigners to him. He was Jewish and they were Macedonians. But Paul did not let any kind of cultural differences bother him. He is a citizen of God's worldwide church, and so are they. He loves them with the love of Jesus.

3. **It was with generosity**. They remember well the way he had lived. He can say to them, *'We were pleased to share with you not only the gospel of God, but also our very lives'* – because he knows they will remember! They will know how hard he worked, how he gave himself to them night and day. He was not bothering about being on holiday in Macedonia! He was not bothering about being a tourist seeing the sights of Macedonia. Far from it. His concern was for them and their need of the good news about Jesus. He knew – and they could remember – that his concern had been nothing other than to be used by God. They had spent time praying with these Thessalonians, answering their questions, making practical suggestions about how the work should continue, being as helpful to them as possible. Paul calls it *'sharing our very lives'*.

What a model Paul is for the Christian. In these days of easy travel, many travelling preachers are more like tourists and holiday-makers than enthusiasts for the good news of Jesus. And what comfortable places they feel 'called' to! But no one could deny the way Paul had lived. When there was criticism, he only had to say 'You remember...!' A few moment's thought was all that was needed for the Thessalonians to recall the sacrificial and dedicated ways of Paul and his friends.

Chapter 7

An Upright Ministry
(1 Thessalonians 2:9–12)

Paul's ministry at Thessalonica had come to a sudden end when he had to abruptly leave the city. Doubts and criticisms were inevitable and Paul was not allowed to return to the city. He had to trust the Holy Spirit to keep the new Christians loyal to Jesus, and he felt he had to send '1 Thessalonians' to give them a true picture of his ministry and of their own recent conversion.

Paul is very open and frank in the way in which he writes. The best way he can defend himself against any doubts they might have about him is simply to remind them of what had happened in Thessalonica and let the facts speak for themselves. He constantly appeals to what they know (see 2:1, 2, 5, 9, 10). He had suffered a lot but is not ashamed of that, and he does not regard suffering as a sign of failure.

He is a steward 'entrusted' with the gospel (2:4). He is an apostle (2:6). He is like a mother (2:7). He is sometimes quite literally a manual labourer (2:8). He is a father (2:11).

Paul oscillates between negative and positive statements, between denials and affirmations. *'It did **not** happen in vain ... we had the boldness in our God to speak to you the gospel ... Our exhortation does **not** come from error ... we speak, **not** to please men but to please God ... And we did **not** seek glory from people ... we were gentle among you ... '.*

Now he puts to them a positive description of what his ministry was like in Thessalonica.

1. **It was a hard-working ministry**. He says, *'For you remember, brothers and sisters, our labour and hardship. We were working night and day, so as not to burden any of you while we proclaimed to you the gospel of God'* (2:9).

Paul was never a burden to the Thessalonians. Often there is nothing wrong with a preacher receiving financial support from those he preaches to. Paul makes this point in 1 Corinthians 9:7–11. But there are situations where it is wise not to make use of that right (as Paul said in 1 Corinthians 9:12). Where a preacher might be suspected of having false motives he would do well to make sure he is not a financial burden upon the people concerned. When Paul was in Thessalonica there was a lot of opposition from the city authorities. Paul could have easily been accused of being a pretender who wanted to exploit people to get money. So he took special care that he could not be accused in that way, and did some manual labour to earn enough to pay his expenses without having to depend on the newly converted Christians in Thessalonica. We may guess that he found out where the local tent-making workers were and got some temporary work with them. Perhaps he preached during the day and did tent-making in the evening. What is certain is that he took care not to be a financial burden on the new Christians. It meant that it was a specially hard-working time for him. The Christians could well remember that this was the way Paul had lived among them during his time in Thessalonica.

2. **It was a ministry of obvious integrity**. He says, *'You yourselves are witnesses and so is God, how godly and upright and blameless was our conduct towards you believers'* (2:10). There was a combination of witnesses to the fact that Paul's life had been straight and upright. They knew, Paul knew, and God knew. He had lived a life of dedication to God (*'godly'*). He had been fair and straight in his dealings with others (*'upright'*). His life had been beyond criticism (*'blameless'*).

3. **It was a fatherly ministry**. *'As you know, we dealt with each one of you like a father with his own children* (2:11),

*exhorting you and encouraging you and testifying to you that
you should walk worthily of God . . . ' (2:12).*

Paul uses many words to describe himself. He is a steward
'entrusted' with the gospel (2:4). He is an apostle (2:6). He is
like a mother (2:7). He is quite literally at times a manual
labourer (2:8). And he is like a father to his new Christian
friends in Thessalonica (2:11).

Paul took care of the new converts at Thessalonica. He
watched over them with the heart of a father caring for his
young children. He *'exhorted them'*, gently pressing upon
them the need to lead a life of godliness. He *'encouraged'*
them, pointing to God's grace and the position that they had
in Jesus which would enable them to walk in newness of life.
He *'testified'* to them, telling them the truth about the life
God wanted them to live. At every point he was like a good
father to them.

4. **It was a ministry with a practical aim in view**. The aim
that Paul had in his work was designed to lead the Thessalonians into lives of godliness. Paul's work was with the
intent that they *'should walk worthily of God who calls you
into his kingdom and glory'* (2:12b).

Once a Christian has come to know Jesus he is to walk
'worthily' – in a way that corresponds to the greatness of
what has happened to him. Christian men and women have
'died' to sin; the power of sin has been broken. They are alive
to God. Then let them walk 'worthily', in a way that fits what
has happened to them.

As the Christian walks in dependence on his new resources
in Jesus, God's call continues. God's call is not simply a call
to our initial salvation. It continues. It is a high calling, a
holy calling. We are being summoned to experience God's
kingly power now in the way in which we live. We are being
changed *'from one degree of glory to another'*, even now in
this life. The whole of Paul's ministry had this practical
purpose in view.

Chapter 8

God's Word

(1 Thessalonians 2:13–16)

Paul had given praise to God for these Thessalonian Christians (1:2–10). Then he went on to speak of his own sincerity (1 Thessalonians 2:1–12). Now he returns to finish his thanksgiving (2:13–16). Paul wants the Thessalonians to get a good perspective on what is happening to them. In these verses his thinking revolves around 'the word', the message about Jesus.

1. **He is grateful that the message concerning Jesus has been recognized**. He says *'And we also thank God constantly for this, that when you received the word of God which you heard from us, you accepted it not as a merely human word, but as what it really is, the word of God'* (2:13a).

The *'word of God'* or *'the word'* is the entire message of Jesus Christ including its implications for our own lives. It can be called *'the word of the kingdom'* (Matthew 13:19), *'the word of God'* (Mark 7:13), *'the word of the Lord'* (Acts 8:25), *'the word of salvation'* (see Acts 13:26), *'the word of grace'* (see Acts 14:3), *'the word of the gospel'* (Acts 15:7), *'the word of reconciliation'* (2 Corinthians 5:19), *'the word of truth'* (Ephesians 1:13), *'the word of life'* (Philippians 2:16), *'the word of Christ'* (Colossians 3:16), *'the word of righteousness'* (Hebrews 5:13) or simply *'the word'* (Luke 1:2).

It is embodied in a person. Jesus is *'the Word'* (John 1:1), the Message revealing God.

It is found in written Scriptures. We have Paul's gospel-message before us in 1 Thessalonians.

It is found in apostolic preaching. The *'word which you heard from us'*, says Paul, is *'the word of God'*.

It is found in modern preaching, but with varying degrees of quality and purity! A modern preacher who preaches the gospel accurately and in the power of the Spirit is delivering *'the word of God'*! Yet Scripture is infallible, and the first generation of apostles were also infallible in their message. The same cannot quite be said of the modern preacher. Yet to the extent that he is faithful to God's written word, to that degree it may be said that his words are God's word. The gospel is not human inventiveness but the message that comes from God concerning Jesus.

2. **Paul is grateful that the message concerning Jesus has internal power**. Paul adds: *'this message is at work in you who believe'*. When a person becomes a Christian 'the word' – the entire message of the gospel – takes up residence in that person's life. There is 'the word' outside of him, the written Scripture and the further teaching that he hears. But there is also 'the word' within as well. Within the Christian's heart there is an instinctive sensitivity to the message of the gospel including its implications for our lives. The gospel message goes on working within. We have to receive with meekness the **implanted** word (James 1:21) which is able progressively to rescue us from the power of sin. Although the Thessalonians might be without the apostle Paul, they are not without 'the word'. It has been planted within them and it goes on working. If Paul is not personally able to get to Thessalonica his presence is not indispensable.

3. **He knows that the message concerning Jesus brings suffering**. There is such a thing as persecution on account of the word (see Mark 4:17). Often people who pretend to have faith abandon what they claim as soon as persecution comes. But the Thessalonians stood strong. *'For you, brothers and sisters, became imitators of the churches of God in Christ Jesus which are in Judea. For you suffered the same things at the hands of your own fellow-countrymen as they suffered from the Jews'* (2:14). Just as there were Jews in Judea who persecuted

Judean Christians, the same thing was happening in Thessalonica. There were Jewish Thessalonians who were persecuting the Christians. The word of God brings persecution. The Christians at Thessalonica must not be troubled by this. They are simply experiencing what Christians have experienced ever since the gospel began to be preached in Judea. *'They killed both the Lord Jesus and the prophets and they drove us out'* (2:15a). The Christians are simply receiving the same treatment that Jesus and the prophets received.

4. **He knows that the message concerning Jesus is protected by God's judgement**. 1 Thessalonians 2:15b–16 is strongly worded. *'They do not please God and they oppose everyone* (2:15b), *by hindering us from speaking to the Gentiles so that Gentiles may be saved. This is so that they, the Jews, may fill up fully the measure of their sins. But wrath has overtaken them utterly'*. Paul has other things to say about Israel and expects them to come to salvation (see Romans 11:25b–26 which must be taken to refer to a nationwide turning to Jesus). Since Paul wrote these words Jews themselves have often been persecuted by Christians caught up in a 'state-church' mentality. Christians **without** the state-church mentality have not persecuted Jews – or anyone else. Early Christians (after Constantine), Christians in the medieval Catholic church, and reformers like Martin Luther all held that there should be a 'state-church'. But any 'state-religion' will persecute!

However the facts are as Paul says. First century Jews hindered the gospel, persecuted Christians, and resorted to all manner of deceit and violence to prevent Jesus from being preached.

Paul's point is that when God's 'word' is opposed, calamity will sooner or later fall on those who use violence to crush God's church. God leaves the persecutor for a while until his sins reach a certain fullness. Then his judgement comes. In the late AD 40s there was famine in Judea that caused great suffering. At passover time in AD 49, Jews were exiled from Rome. In the AD 60s relationship with the Roman empire deteriorated. In the late AD 60s Roman soldiers marched on Jerusalem. In AD 70 the city was destroyed and for decades Jerusalem was a derelict city.

In the AD 50s Paul sees the matter from God's viewpoint. *'Wrath has overtaken them utterly'*. God's word gets protected; justice falls on a persecutor eventually.

Chapter 9

The Preacher's Crown

(1 Thessalonians 2:17–20)

Paul turns again in 1 Thessalonians 2:17–3:13 to talk about his concern for the Thessalonians and his relations with them.

His wish to return to them had been frustrated (2:17–20). So he had sent Timothy (3:1–5) and was encouraged by the news Timothy brought back (3:6–11).

When Paul left Thessalonica, after establishing the church, he had been forced to leave the city and his friend Jason had to guarantee that Paul would leave quietly and not return (Acts 17:9). It was difficult for Paul. He had only been at Thessalonica for a short time. A small but lively church had come into being, yet Paul could not go back to see them.

1. **Paul loved personal contact; this was a very important part of his ministry**. He speaks very strongly about the matter; he does not want anyone to think that he had any choice. If it had been possible to stay longer at Thessalonica he would have stayed. *'And we, brothers and sisters, when we were deprived of your company for a short time – out of sight but not out of our affection – we were greatly longing with immense eagerness to see you face to face* (2:17). *So we wanted to come to you. I, Paul, wanted to come, again and again...'* (2:18).

This is a vital aspect of Christian ministry and fellowship: person-to-person contact and sharing, close praying with

39

brothers and sisters, individual knowledge and observation of what is happening in each others' lives. Although each Christian man or woman needs time to think and pray alone, and there are some things we should keep to ourselves (see Romans 14:5, 12, 22) yet for much of the time our need is for good fellowship and personal contact. Paul was able to send letters to the Christians at Thessalonica; he sent what we call '1 Thessalonians', and he could send Timothy (see 3:2). But the great desire of his heart was to be with his brothers and sisters in person.

2. **He regarded a break in personal contact as the opposition of Satan**. He did not think that it was simply the will of God. *'I, Paul, wanted to come, again and again, but Satan hindered us'*. This is a very important phrase: *'... but Satan hindered us'*. Does this mean that Satan defeated Paul? Does this mean that God did not get victory at this particular point of Paul's ministry?

When something bad happens in the spiritual world, who is doing it – God or Satan? Could Paul have said 'I, Paul, wanted to come, again and again, but it was not God's will'? Could he have said this? Look at Romans 1:9–13.

When something bad happens in the spiritual world, it is Satan doing it and it is God permitting it. You could say 'Satan did it.' You could say 'God allowed it.' It was Satan who attacked Job, yet we know that Satan could do nothing without God's permission. So it was Satan's will to attack Job, and it was God's will to let him!

Can Satan ever defeat a godly man or woman? Yes – temporarily. But then the victory ends up being greater than ever. Did Satan defeat Jesus on the cross? It looked like it and Satan thought so. But actually in the very 'defeat' of the cross Jesus was giving a public example of Satan's defeat and triumphing over him (see Colossians 2:15).

Satan and God may be involved in the same event, but what God is doing is not the same as what Satan is doing. Satan attacks to weaken and destroy. God gives him permission in order to make us stronger. Satan wants to knock us down; God wants to build us up.

So sometimes God allows the devil to have his way in

order to achieve something yet greater than anyone expected. The devil stopped Paul going to Thessalonica, but as a result the church of Jesus got 1 Thessalonians! Job said at the end of his experience: *'No purpose of yours can be thwarted!'* (Job 42:2). Satan is not always defeated at the beginning but he is always defeated in the end. He may win a battle but he has lost the war.

But Paul knew the devil was involved in the obstruction to his returning to Thessalonica. He was living on principles, and he knew as a matter of principle that personal contact with God's people was what was needed. If it was being blocked it was Satan who was involved.

3. **Paul knew that his reward in heaven was connected with his ministry**. Paul has already spoken about the Christian's 'hope', his expectation of blessing that arises from faith in Jesus (1:3). The Christians are eagerly looking forward to Jesus' coming (1:10). Paul and the Christians at Thessalonica are being called *'into his kingdom and glory'* (2:12). This hope is stored up in heaven. Paul does not say heaven is the hope; he likes to speak of something stored up 'in' heaven (see Colossians 1:5). He is expecting to *'reap back from the Spirit'* (Galatians 6:8) blessings from God in this world; he also expects a heavenly reward beyond the grave. Faithfulness to Jesus will result in great joy beyond death, and a crown in which his faithfulness will be visible. This is his 'helmet' which makes him hold his head high (5:8); it comes at the final stage of salvation (5:8, 9).

But what is the reward? It has a lot to do with our work being publicly seen as blessed by God; every Christian has some calling within the church of Jesus and it will one day become visible. *'For what is our hope or joy or crown before our Lord Jesus at his coming? Is it not you'* (2:19)? The Thessalonians themselves are tied together with Paul. *'For you are our glory and our joy'* (2:20). Each Christian has some calling within the church of Jesus Christ. Every Christian will personally stand before Jesus Christ at the time of Jesus' coming. Each one of us will receive praise or blame before Jesus. Unforgiven sins will be exposed. What receives God's praise will be the extent to which we have turned many to righteousness. They that have turned many to righteousness and helped keep them safe in Jesus will shine like the brightness of the heavens. Our fellow Christians are our reward!

Chapter 10

Watching Over New Christians
(1 Thessalonians 3:1–5)

Paul has a strong and definite doctrine of predestination, as we have seen in 1 Thessalonians 1:4. There is no explaining it away! Yet it is also true that Paul has a strong sense of responsibility and of the serious consequences of what we do.

1. We can observe Paul's deep **sense of responsibility** for new Christians. He was deeply concerned with the need to care for these recently converted men and women in Thessalonica. He was not able simply to say 'God will take care of them. If they are truly saved, they will endure for ever. All will be well!' His doctrine of predestination was not over-logical, or fatalistic. He could not simply leave them to God. He felt that he himself was responsible for what happened to these young Christians. Paul had a very deep longing to know how they were doing and what was happening to them. He left them only because he was forced to leave them (2:17a) and he tried to get back to them (2:17b–20). Finally he felt he had no choice but to send Timothy back. *'So when we could endure it no longer we thought it good to be left behind at Athens alone...'* (3:1). Paul simply had to know what was happening to these young Christians. The suspense of not knowing what was happening to them was agony for him. Finally he felt he had to endure the painful experience of being left alone and that he would have to send Timothy. He says *'...and we sent Timothy our brother and God's fellow-worker in the gospel of Christ...'*.

43

Why was it so painful for Paul to be left behind? One must realise the situation. It was not like being left behind in a modern capital city with its hotels and shops and its many comforts. Athens was a wicked and an idolatrous city. It was very painful for Paul to be totally alone in such a place. Yet his sense of responsibility was so great; he was willing to endure isolation as a stranger in a dangerous place rather than not know what was happening to the new Christians he had left behind.

2. We can observe Paul's **realisation that Christian ministry is being a co-worker with God**. He calls Timothy *'God's fellow worker'*. It is a surprising phrase. We would expect him to say 'my fellow worker'. But Paul had to send Timothy to Thessalonica not knowing precisely what he would find. Paul was sure God would lead him. God would reveal what he should say and do, and how he would relate to the Thessalonians. Paul trusted that God would be at work in Timothy's life. He had often been a co-worker with Paul but at this point it was not his working with Paul that mattered. What would count as he went back without Paul is his being able to be led by God. Paul is confident. Timothy is the kind of person who works with God. This is what Christian work consists of: being a co-worker with God.

3. We can observe Paul's **concern to promote strength and maturity**. Paul had several concerns on his heart for these new Christians. He tells the Thessalonians he sent Timothy (i) *'to establish you and encourage you in your faith* (3:2), *in case anyone should be moved by these afflictions. For this is something we are appointed to!'* (3:3). Young Christians in an atmosphere of such heavy opposition need to be established by those like Timothy who have behind them years in which they have proved the faithfulness of God. The young Christians being persecuted need to be helped to become steady and constant amidst the antagonism from the people of Thessalonica. They need encouraging in faith.

Then he also wants Timothy (ii) to help them to face the fact that the Christian life has many tribulations in it. Paul had already told them this. *'For even when we were with you we told you beforehand that we would suffer affliction. So indeed it has happened and you know about it'* (3:4). There are versions of the Christian faith which avoid mention of this. The impression is sometimes given that a true believer will not have tribulation but will live a life of easy prosperity. Paul is more honest and realistic. He goes out of his way to warn young Christians right at the beginning of their new life that they must be ready and willing to face adversity. God is with them amidst tribulations, but He is not always in a hurry to pull us out of tribulations.

(iii) Thirdly, Paul sent Timothy to protect them against Satan. He says, *'This is the reason why, when I could no longer bear it I also sent to get to know about your faith in case somehow the tempter had tempted you and our work should be profitless'* (3:5). One part of Paul's sense of responsibility was his awareness of Satan. The devil loves to discourage and to lead a new Christian into something that will ruin his or her life. Paul is ever alert to the need of rescuing the Christian who is about to fall into discouragement, false teaching or some piece of extremism. If Satan's attack is extreme and the young Christian is not sent help, the new baby-in-the-Lord can be ruined right from the start. Paul's aim is not simply to get people to profess faith. He did not reckon he had achieved much unless the young Christian came through to steadfastness and maturity. If the new convert fell by the wayside under the attacks of Satan, Paul maintained his work had been done 'in vain'. It had not been followed through to its desired end. So he watched over his new Christian friends *'in case somehow . . . our work should be profitless'* (3:5).

Our responsibility to young Christians is great.

Chapter 11

Persistent Faith

(1 Thessalonians 3:6–10)

Paul took very seriously the need to assist Christians after they had come to faith in Jesus. It gave him grave anxiety if he was not able to continue to see new believers.

1. **Paul took a lot of trouble to keep a warm relationship with his new friends**. Timothy came back to Paul at Athens and brought the good news that the Thessalonians were continuing in faith towards God and in love among each other, and they were still holding on to their love of Paul as the one who had been the messenger of God to them. Paul was overjoyed. He lived for the progress of his converts and nothing gave him greater peace and joy than to see them progressing firmly. Soon after Timothy arrived he wrote 1 Thessalonians. *'But now Timothy has come to us from you and has brought us the good news of your faith and your love. He has told us that you always think well of us, and that you want to see us just as we also long to see you'* (3:6).

He wrote as soon as he got the news. He did not want his relationship with them to get cold. His language is warm and appreciative. He wants the Thessalonians to know how much he feels for them and loves them. They are new people in his life. He has not known them for very long. But he has taken them into his heart and expresses his great love for them as speedily as he can after receiving the news about them.

2. **The great need of the young Christian is to persevere in faith**. It can be seen that what Paul is concerned about is that

the Thessalonians should continue to believe. It is faith and love (in that order!) that he wants to see. *'For this reason'*, he says, referring to their faith and love, *'in all our distress and suffering we have been encouraged by the news about you, brothers and sisters, especially by the news of your faith'* (3:7). Paul himself had suffered. The furious mob in Thessalonica that attacked the house where Paul was staying (Acts 17:5), the hurried expulsion from the city (Acts 17:10), the isolation in an idolatrous city (Acts 17:16), were all exceedingly stressful for him. But it would be worth it all if the Thessalonians came through as firm believers – and that is what happened!

It is obvious that Paul is particularly concerned to know of their faith. Some only pretend to believe. The first piece of trouble that comes along makes them abandon any claim to believe. 'I tried it and it did not work,' they say, when actually there is no faith in their heart. So Paul is very eager to know that they are still believing. There is a further reason why Paul looks for on-going faith in the Thessalonians. The Christian has to learn to apply his faith amidst the troubles of life. It is one thing to believe in Jesus as the Saviour, but fruitfulness in the Christian life is the result of **persistent** faith.

3. **Paul gets his joy from seeing persistent faith in his people**. His sadness and his joy are affected by this. Will these people continue to believe amidst all of the pressures that are going to come upon them in Thessalonica? No real blessing will come into their lives unless they **persist** in faith. Paul can hardly wait to know whether they are still going on in faith despite the great opposition they are facing. It is this that is causing Paul such agony. But all is well. *'We have been encouraged by the news about you . . . especially by the news of your faith'*. He goes on, *'For now we are really alive if you are standing firm in the Lord'* (3:8). Paul gets vibrant energy and joy from the knowledge that his new Christians friends are standing firm in faith. This is the source of his joy and it intensifies his thanksgiving to God. *'For what thanksgiving can we give to God in return for you? What thanks can we give for the joy that we have because of you, in the presence of our God . . . ?'* (3:9).

This is the kind of 'success' Paul is looking for. It is one of his greatest ambitions: to see those people for whom he has responsibility before God continuing to believe.

4. **Paul knows that there is more work to be done in building up his new friends in the Lord Jesus**. He needs to see more of them. He makes it a matter of prayer. What thanks can we have ... *'while night and day we pray very intensely that we may see you face to face and may supply what is lacking in your faith?'* What a great man of prayer Paul was! He prays for hours, often in the middle of the night. The phrase he uses is a very strong one. He and his friends pray *'most earnestly'* or *'with all our heart'*.

The reason for this very intense praying is that he knows that although their faith is real there is something lacking in it. It needs filling out. It needs to develop determination, resolution and rich knowledge of the faithfulness of God. They must learn to handle themselves as Christian people amidst a wicked world. They need to develop godliness, brotherly affection, and a loving graciousness to all people everywhere. They are young Christians. In this sense there is 'something lacking' in their faith.

Paul has to find ways of meeting their need. Teaching them in a face-to-face situation is what he wants to do the most, but meanwhile his letter – our 1 Thessalonians – will be a start. Certainly there is more work to be done. Those who have any kind of pastoral ministry have to build people up in Christian godliness. Conversion is only the beginning.

Chapter 12

Preparing for Jesus' Coming
(1 Thessalonians 3:11–13)

In 1 Thessalonians we are seeing how Paul worked as an apostle. He loved personal contact with people (2:17–18) and took steps to ensure the care of those who had just come to faith (3:1–5). Although he was forced to endure much opposition, he did a lot of 'follow-up' with his new Christians, strengthening them (3:2), and encouraging them in troubles (3:3–5). He made it a principle of his life to accept continuing responsibility for those he brought to faith (3:6–10).

Yet another principle that governed Paul's life appears in 3:11–13: the responsibility to pray for those to whom we minister.

We all need these principles, because although we are not apostles quite like Paul we all have *'gifts that differ'* (Romans 12:6) and are to use them in the church of Jesus Christ. All Christians have *'grace given according to the measure of Christ's gift'* (Ephesians 4:7). Not every Christian is a preacher but every Christian has a testimony about Jesus, and every Christian is a 'minister' in one way or another. He or she 'ministers' or 'serves' among God's people.

1. **Paul makes his future plans a matter of prayer**. He turns his thoughts to God. *'Now may our God and Father himself, and our Lord Jesus, direct our way to you'* (3:11). He is praying to God the Father, and he is praying to Jesus. The Father and the Son are equally divine. He hopes that God

will give him a straight and speedy journey to see the Thessalonians. God the Father is God. Jesus is God. We can pray to the Father. We can pray to the Son of God, Jesus. So Paul asks *'our God and Father himself, and our Lord Jesus'* to guide him at this time.

2. **Paul's prayer specially asks for the increase of love among his new Christian friends**. Love is the greatest height of Christian living. Paul prays *'and may the Lord make you increase and abound in love to one another and to all people, as also we have love for you'*. The Christian life begins with faith but it works out in love. When we are seeking to live a godly life we focus on the life of love more than on anything else. Then we look to see our love increasing. This is what Paul prays for. The Thessalonians have begun; Paul is looking for greater heights of love among them.

He himself seeks to be a good example to them. He wants them to show Christian love *'as also we have love for you'*.

Paul distinguishes between love among the Christians and love for everyone everywhere. We need to give attention to both. Sometimes it is easier to love people outside the church than those we are close to. This is not because the world is very lovable. It is because we are closer to our friends in the church. It is generally difficult to show love to people we are closest to.

3. **Love will lead to perfection in holiness**. Of course Christian 'perfection' is not sinlessness. We never get to the point where we have no more growing to do in the Christian life. We never get to the point where we are as holy as Jesus was when He lived on earth. We never get to the point where we do not need the blood of Jesus to wash us clean every day.

But Christian love does lead to what Paul calls being 'complete'. *'This will lead to his strengthening your hearts for being perfect in holiness before God and our Father at the coming of our Lord Jesus with all his holy people'* (3:13). This 'perfection' is not absolute sinlessness but it is having every area of our lives basically right. It is all-round sincerity and genuineness. It is being the kind of person where the world has no right to criticize – although it will anyway!

Love strengthens our hearts! It results in our being more

determined to live for God, more aware of God's presence, more able to endure amidst trial. Our inner life gets more resolute, more assured of God's love for us, more confident and happy in living for God. Love is something which we need to diligently seek from God. Paul makes growth in love a matter of prayer, and so should we, both for ourselves and for others. It will do a lot for us!

4. **Continuing in love makes us ready for the Second Coming of Jesus**. Paul says that love will lead to our inner life being strengthened so that there is an all-round godliness and we are ready for *'the coming of our Lord Jesus with all his holy people'*.

Love gets us ready for the Second Coming of Jesus. Jesus is going to come again, visibly, gloriously, majestically. It will be a time when everyone will be seen for what he or she really is. Much of our life now is hidden or misunderstood. Godly people do much for the Lord in secret. Wicked people do much of their sinning in secret. But the day of Jesus' appearing will be the day when everything else appears as well.

Paul wants us to be *'perfect in holiness ... at the coming of our Lord Jesus'*. It is not total sinlessness, but it is being ready for Jesus to interview us. The question is: what level of godliness will we have reached at the time when Jesus comes? If Jesus were to come today, what level of love would he find in us? Jesus may come at any moment, in one way or another. Even if his final coming is delayed, as it may well be, he has other ways of 'coming'. There are times when it is as if God comes to investigate how we are doing. *'The Lord came down to see ... '*, says Genesis 11:5. *'I will go down now, and see ... '*, says Genesis 18:21. There are times – even before the final coming of Jesus – when God 'comes'. God wants us always – even if Jesus' coming is to be delayed – to be ready for Jesus to come, ready for God to investigate us. There will be blessing or judgement, honour or disgrace, when Jesus comes. And in one way or another Jesus' coming is always sooner and more unexpected than we imagined. Love gets us ready.

Chapter 13

The Call to Holiness

(1 Thessalonians 4:1–4)

Paul has finished his praying, praising and looking back to the time when the Thessalonian church started. Now he makes a turn in his letter and begins to directly appeal to the Christians to live a godly life. He appeals for holiness generally (4:1–3a), then for sexual purity (4:3b–8), for a life of love (4:9–10 and hard work (4:11–12).

Some general points worth making are these.

1. **The Christian preacher is to be concerned about godliness**. In every letter Paul writes, his concern is about godliness. This is what Christian faith is all about. It is not a prosperity movement. It is not a social club. It is not a commercial business or a financial campaign. It is not an entertainment centre. It is not a philosophy looking for the truth.

What then is the Christian faith? Among other things it is a holiness movement. It starts by saving us and bringing us into relationship with God. Then it lifts us up into high levels of godliness and spirituality. The church is a campaign headquarters in the battle for godliness.

Sooner or later in every New Testament letter the apostles will get to the subject of holiness in the lives of their people.

2. **Holiness is not taught in a mistaken way**. It is worth noting what Paul does not do.

He does not appeal to them to have a 'holiness' experience.

He does not appeal to them to have a 'deliverance' experience. He does not say to them, 'You have come to salvation but now you need deliverance.' No biblical writer says anything like that.

He does not tell them they need the law of Sinai. He does not put the Thessalonians under the Mosaic law. He does not expound a detailed list of regulations. The world's way of appealing for morality or good living is quite different from God's way. The world is concerned about its rights and its pleasures. It sometimes tries to produce a certain amount of good living in other people. It is concerned (sometimes!) about ethics and good living.

When the world is concerned about good living it generally turns to laws. You must do this and you must not do that! The biblical way is different.

3. **Paul's method of holiness teaching is to tell the Christians to work out what they already have in Jesus**. It is only Christian people that he asks to live a godly life. He does not appeal to the world to be godly. He appeals to the world to get saved and to the Christians to work out their salvation. Paul has spent three chapters of 1 Thessalonians getting the Christians to see what happened to them when they first came to salvation. Then, after he has done that, he appeals to them to live godly lives. They are to live under the leading of Jesus. They are to walk in the Spirit. Paul appeals to the relationship he and they have with Jesus. *'We urge ... in the Lord Jesus ... '*.

He is friendly and encouraging. *'And coming to another matter, brothers and sisters, we ask you and appeal to you in the Lord Jesus that as you received from us instruction about how you should live your life and how you should please God (as you are in fact doing) that you may excel still more'* (4:1). He calls them *'brothers and sisters'*. He simply *'urges'* and *'exhorts'* them. He commends them for their obedience so far (*'as you are in fact doing'* – omitted by KJV).

Although the Christian life is lived *'in the Spirit'* it is not vague and undefined. Paul has given them instructions (*'as you received instruction ... '*) and he is about to give them more instructions. It is possible to state what God demands and talk about it. One can describe the kind of life the Spirit leads us into. There is such a thing as obligation and duty. Paul is concerned about our actual life, our 'walk'. The Christian life is a matter of pleasing or displeasing God. (*'how you should please God...'*). It is a matter of growth (*'... excel still more...'*). Paul has spoken about this before. He says: *'for you know what instructions we gave you through the Lord Jesus'* (4:2). He knows that this is something God is very serious about. *'For this is the wish of God; it is for your sanctification'* (4:3a).

4. **Eventually Paul gives very precise instruction**. He does not begin with regulations or demands. He tells them their position in Jesus Christ (1 Thessalonians chapters 1–3). Then he gives a general appeal letting them know the demand for godliness is a serious matter. Then he gets down to details.

He starts with a call for purity (4:3b–8). He first speaks to them negatively: they must abstain from immorality (4:3b). He says *'He* – God – *requires that you abstain from sexual immorality...'* (4:3b).

Is it necessary for Paul to say this? Yes! The sexual drive is strong in most people. Their past sins may still tempt them. Friends and colleagues exert pressure. Slow backsliding may lead into very serious playing around with sin.

Is this a special problem to you? What should you do if it is? (i) Grasp your position in Jesus. Before you do anything, receive forgiveness and rejoice in the Lord. (ii) If you are in the grip of this, cry out to God. Ask him to give you special help. The answer may come in the form of suffering. It often takes suffering to break the power of sin. 'Fear of the Lord' is the knowledge of the suffering that might come.

Walk in the Spirit. Avoid situations which lead you into sin. Focus on positively serving God. Reckon you have died to the dominion of sin. Know that you are indeed alive in Jesus. Walk in newness of life. Rejoice in God so much that sin is weakened. You can live this way.

Chapter 14

Honouring the Body

(1 Thessalonians 4:4–8)

Paul gets increasingly detailed as he presses upon the Thessalonians the need to live a godly life. He is not giving a book of regulations. The Spirit will help them as they seek to live a life of detailed godliness. Yet in addition to the Holy Spirit we often need a Christian friend or pastor to give us some words of exhortation, and that is what Paul is doing.

1. **Paul urges that we give honour and dignity to the body**. God requires that we *'abstain from sexual immorality...'* (4:3b). In verse 4 some translations have *'that each of you knows how to take a wife'*. There is a word which might mean 'take' or 'gain control', and another which might mean 'body' or 'wife'. But *'gain control over his or her body'* is surely the better translation. Paul speaks of *'each of you'* and so is writing to every Thessalonian Christian; not simply to unmarried men! The women do not need to be told how to take a wife! Paul is surely writing to them too. So the translation must be *'... that each of you knows how to use his or her body in holiness and in honour...'* (4:4).

It is not just a matter of sexual purity. That is part of the matter but there is more. We are to keep our bodies in holiness and honour in every way. We are to have a kind of pride in one's body. This involves concern about our health and fitness, concern about decent appearance, cleanliness, hygiene. Sexual experience is to be kept within the context of marriage. Our weight is to be maintained at a sensible level, and so on. Some ancient philosophies despised the body, but the apostles urged the Christians to glorify God in their bodies!

2. **Paul urges the Christians to maintain sexual purity**. Part of this giving value and dignity to the body is that sexual purity becomes an inflexible habit. Paul continues: '... *not in lustful passion like the pagan nations who do not know God'* (4:5). One notices how he uses a Christian way of appealing to them. He is not simply threatening them with disease or danger. He says 'You now know God! The pagans must be expected to live their wicked lives, for they do not know God, but you Christians do know God. Put your knowledge of God into practise. Rejoice in God so much that you live a different kind of life from that which the pagans live.'

3. **Paul specially urges care in sexual purity within the Christian fellowship**. The Thessalonians are young Christians and are being persecuted by the pagans around them. Paul has been urging them to show affection to one another and it will be natural for them to draw together as a close fellowship standing against the opposition of the world around them. Any wrong relationships with the opposite sex could possibly be within the very fellowship of the Thessalonians. It is this that leads Paul to add a warning about purity of relationships within the Christian fellowship. He says *'do not go beyond what is proper and defraud in this matter a brother or sister ...'*. He is still referring to sexual relationships. It would be 'defrauding a brother or sister' to be setting up a wrong sexual relationship with another person of the fellowship. The Christian is not to steal another person's partner.

4. **Paul gives specifically Christian reasons for his appeal in these matters**. Again we note that what Paul says could not be said to an unconverted person. Paul's appeal is especially to things that Christians believe in. He says Christian purity is needed '... *because the Lord is an avenger concerning all of these things – as also we said to you before and testified'* (4:6). A first reason for care is that the Christian knows that God is likely to act in justice at any time. The transgressor may not have to wait till judgement day. God might act at any moment in severe chastening.

A second reason for conscientiousness in this matter is put next: *'for God did not call us to uncleanness but in sanctification'* (4:7). The Christian is 'called' to holiness. The Christian's salvation comes by God's 'call'. God works powerfully in our hearts bringing us to salvation, getting us to see things we could not see by nature, strongly drawing us to Jesus. But the Christian's calling does not stop at our first conversion. It continues. God is still calling us. It is an upward calling, a high calling, a calling to sanctification, to ministry, to heavenly reward.

So to neglect the call to purity is to resist the very thing God has been doing in our lives ever since our first conversion.

On the other hand God's calling to holiness is very encouraging. If God is calling us we must be able to achieve what He is calling us to. His call is accompanied by his enabling.

A third reason for taking seriously Paul's challenges is found in 4:8, *'Therefore, the person who rejects this instruction rejects not man but God, who gives the Holy Spirit to you'*. It is dangerous to sin in this way because of the authority of the Holy Spirit within us. Every aspect of the work of the Spirit within us is designed to help us in the pathway of godliness. The 'leading of the Spirit' is leading in the pathway of purity. The Holy Spirit prompts us to walk in the ways of righteousness. He convicts us when we wander into ways of sin. As Paul writes these words, the Christian knows Paul is right. By the Spirit, the works of the flesh are obvious. We do not need some special revelation to know that these paths of impurity are displeasing to God. We know it. To resist Paul's instruction is to resist the Holy Spirit's work within us.

Chapter 15

Love and Labour

(1 Thessalonians 4:9–12)

Christian salvation involves conversion to a life of practical godliness. The Thessalonians have not been Christians very long, but Paul expects them already to be living a life of purity (4:3b–8).

1. **Now he asks them to live a life of love** (4:9–10). For Paul, love does not require a lot of legislation. The Thessalonians know what love is. *'Now concerning love of the brothers and sisters you do not have need of our writing to you, for you yourselves are taught by God to love one another...'* (4:9). God himself works directly in the heart of the saved person. By the Holy Spirit he or she knows what it means to love. As soon as they came to salvation, and without much teaching, the Thessalonians began to practise love towards each other. The more God works in us, the more the side-effects of love are created within us.

Paul can point to the evidence: *'...and you do show brotherly love for all the brothers and sisters throughout Macedonia'* (4:10a). Paul is using two words here *'brotherly love'* (4:9) and the ordinary New Testament word, *'love'*. The two are closely linked. There is *'brotherly love'* – love that is produced because someone is specially close to us as our brother or sister. And there is *'love'*, the undeserved love towards others that dwells within us by God's Spirit.

They already know what it means to love. All Paul can ask is that it should grow and become multiplied: *'Yet we urge*

58

you brothers and sisters to do so more and more . . . ' (4:10b).
Love has to endlessly grow. What might this mean in practice? How might we see that we are growing in Christian
love? It would mean that we are less and less critical, more
and more affectionate, more practical in the ways we are
helpful to others. It would mean that we put down others less
and we build up others more. It would mean that we become
more observant about other's weaknesses and would seek
increasingly to give them help and support in those areas
of weakness. It would mean that we give them an ever-
increasing sense that they are accepted by us, and that we
hold no grudges or resentments against them. It would mean
that we increasingly learn to cope with the unlovely, for not
everyone in the fellowship will easily draw out our love. It
would mean that we cease to bother about defending
ourselves (because such self-defence damages love).

Paul is particularly concerned with love within the Christian fellowship. While Christians are called upon to love
everyone everywhere, we also have a special calling to
produce a community of love which attracts the world and
shows them that we have what they need. It is by love that
the world gets to know that we are Jesus' disciples.

2. **He asks them to live a steady life** (4:11–12). He is
concerned about a group of people in the church at Thessalonica who he calls (5:14) *'disorderly'* or *'unruly'*. In many
Christian fellowships there are likely to be people who like
excitement more than they like discipline. They like things to
be happening to them rather than to work in such a way that
they get good things to happen! Such people always get very
excited by the doctrine of the Second Coming of Jesus, and
they tend to start making wild predictions. They are also in
danger of neglecting very ordinary duties in the Christian
life because of their excitement about predictions and
prophecies. They are disorderly, idle, and like to meddle in
other peoples' lives rather than get on with their 'ordinary'
Christian responsibilities.

Paul urges the Christians to show love more and more,
*'and to make it an ambition to live calmly, to see to your own
responsibilities and to work with your hands, as we urged you*

(4:11). *One purpose in this is that you may behave decently towards outsiders, and may have need of nothing'* (4:12).

'Make it an ambition to live calmly'. Paul says 'if you want to make a fuss about something, make a fuss about learning to calm down!' They had been getting so excited about the Second Coming of Jesus, that they were getting ready for it as if it were tomorrow morning. It happens often. People begin to get worked up about prophecies and predictions and they start becoming a nuisance and neglecting the 'ordinary' aspects of the Christian life.

'Make it an ambition to live calmly!' The Christian must not be an over-excited person. He must not exaggerate the teaching about the Second Coming – or about anything else in the Bible. People get into the same kind of excitement about other matters also: health and wealth, predictions about their country, what marvellous prophecies God has given about their lives, how God has given them a great ministry for this or for that . . . ! But there often creeps in a kind of super-excitement that does not last very long and leads to disillusionment in the end.

'See to your own responsibilities'. Most early Christians were quite poor, so these people did not have major responsibilities as prominent citizens. Paul tells them to be willing to do some manual labour. They must find a way of providing for themselves and not be dependent on other Christians to pay for their needs.

If they live in this way, those outside the Christian fellowship will see that the people of Jesus are sensible people. A Christian who is half-fanatic and half-beggar does damage to the gospel. The Christians' willingness to work will impress others as they see we live in a balanced way and *'have need of nothing'.*

Chapter 16

The Second Coming of Jesus
(1 Thessalonians 4:13–15)

Paul now comes to one particular matter that was troubling the Thessalonians. Paul had obviously taught them about Jesus' Second Coming when he had been with them in Thessalonica, and it appears that the Thessalonians had exaggerated his teaching. They began to be quite dogmatic that the Second Coming of Jesus would come very soon, certainly within the lifetime of every Thessalonian Christian.

Paul **hoped** to be alive at the time of Jesus' Second Coming. He would have encouraged the Thessalonians to have the same hope. In 4:15 he speaks of *'we who are alive, who are left until the coming of the Lord'*; and in 4:17 of *'we who are alive, who are left'*. He certainly was optimistic about being alive at the time of Jesus' coming. But it is one thing to speak optimistically and it is another thing to make dogmatic statements about when the Second Coming will be. Paul did not know. He could only speak hopefully.

The Thessalonians were quite dogmatic that the Second Coming of Jesus would be soon, within their lifetime. But then some of the elderly Thessalonians died – and that gave the Thessalonians difficulties. Had these people who had died sinned especially? Was God punishing them? Would they miss the final glory that would come when Jesus returned?

1. **The Christian may have great encouragement in the face of death**. Paul gives some help to his grieving friends at Thessalonica. *'Now we want you to know the truth, brothers*

61

and sisters, about those who have died, so that you will not grieve as others do who have no hope' (4:13). Paul wants them to be well-informed about this matter. A clear grasp of the teaching will deliver them from excessive grief.

The phrase *'those who have died'* is literally *'those who have fallen asleep'*. One should not use the phrase *'fallen asleep'* to try to establish any particular teaching about life after death. It does not (for example) mean that the soul is 'asleep' after death. The phrase is simply a 'euphemism' (a nice way of speaking). Like a person asleep, those who have died take no part in **this** world. The phrase can be used of a bad king, like Ahab (1 Kings 22:40). It was used in Greek writings even before the New Testament period.

2. **Death does not rob anyone of the blessings of the Second Coming of Jesus**. They need not worry about Christians who have died. *'For since we believe that Jesus died and rose again, we also believe that God will bring back those have fallen asleep with Jesus'* (4:14). The anxiety of the Thessalonians is not whether these Christians have gone to heaven or to hell. Their anxiety, to be precise, concerns whether the Christians who have died have missed out on the glorious event of Jesus' Second Coming. Paul says 'No. God will bring them back for the occasion!'

Believers who have died will be physically raised from the dead. The reason for believing this is that believers are united to Jesus. What has happened to Jesus will happen to them. Jesus died, but that was not the end. He rose again in the body. Christians are in Christ. They too may die. But they too will rise again. If we believe one, we should believe in the other. If we believe in Jesus' death and resurrection, we should believe in the Christian's death and resurrection. The basis of Christian safety is that all Christians are united with Jesus Christ.

I generally avoid technicalities but there are some here that cannot be avoided. One question is: where does *'through Jesus'* or *'with Jesus'* belong? Is it *'God will* **through Jesus** *bring back with him...'*? Or is it *'those who have died* **with Jesus'** – that is *'those who have died but have been united by faith to Jesus Christ'*. The second is the most likely.[1] *'God will* *bring back those who have fallen asleep with Jesus'* – those who were Christians.

Another question is: the text says *'God will **lead** those who have fallen asleep . . . '*. Does this mean *'God will **take back** . . . those who have died'* (as the Good News Bible has it)? Or does it mean *'God will **bring** back with Jesus those who have died'*? Is the word *'take back'* or *'bring back'*? Almost certainly it means 'will bring back'.[2]

3. **Those who have died will not be overlooked at the Second Coming of Jesus**. Paul now lays down some clear teaching. *'For this we declare to you by the word of the Lord, that we who are alive, who are left until the coming of the Lord, shall not go ahead of those who have fallen asleep'* (4:15). Paul's teaching comes by *'the word of the Lord'*. The 'Lord' is Jesus. Apparently it was known to the early Christian exactly what Jesus had taught on this subject. A 'word of the Lord' is a saying or piece of teaching from Jesus handed down by the Jerusalem church. (Note 1 Corinthians 7:12 where Paul used his own apostolic inspiration but had no saying of Jesus to quote.)

The teaching is that those who are alive when Jesus comes will not have any advantages over those who have died. Those who have died will not be left aside. God will raise them from the dead and they will be present when Jesus reveals his divine glory. If Jesus comes soon we shall see Jesus come. But we shall not 'go ahead' of those who have died. They will be brought back for the occasion!

Footnotes

[1] Otherwise the word 'bring' is heavily weighted with attaching phrases. Also the aorist tense of *koimethentas* suggests that it means 'those who have died in fellowship with Jesus'.

[2] The phrase is 'lead with him' and the Christian does not literally die at the same time Jesus died, but he does literally return at the same time Jesus returns. Verse 14 goes on to deal with the return of Jesus. All of this points to the meaning 'bring back with him'.

Chapter 17

Resurrection and Rapture

(1 Thessalonians 4:16–18)

The Thessalonians evidently thought that only living believers would be involved in the Second Coming. Paul says 'No. Believers who have died will be raised to take part in the Second Coming of Jesus.'

Paul now describes the Second Coming of Jesus. First, Jesus himself will descend from heaven. *'For the Lord himself will descend from heaven with a cry of command, with an archangel's call, and with the sound of the trumpet of God'* (4:16a).

It is worth noting that **there is only one Second Coming**! The idea that the 'rapture' is different from the Second Coming of Jesus is taught nowhere in the Bible. There is not a Second Coming and a Third Coming! The Thessalonians are looking forward to one event, the one-and-only Second Coming of Jesus. The idea that there will be one coming, followed by seven years, followed by another coming is simply not in the Bible, although some good people have believed it since the idea was started in about 1830. Hebrews 9:28 speaks of Jesus' appearing *'a second time'*. There is a one-and-only Second Coming of Jesus, not a two-stage coming.

1. **There is a return**. Jesus himself will descend from heaven. He will come personally, visibly, gloriously. The shout is a powerful shout of command. Jesus himself shouts 'Come forth!' as He did outside the tomb of Lazarus (John 11:43–44). The archangel's call suggests that the angelic

64

world is rejoicing in the victory of Jesus and that sin is at last about to be judged. The trumpet of God is an announcement that the people of God are about to move forward a stage in their story. (Trumpet calls were used to mark the moving forward of an army or a pilgrim people.) God himself issues a trumpet call to his people to make their last move towards home.

We notice that this Second Coming is a noisy event, a visible event, a public event. There is certainly no 'secret rapture' here.

2. **There is a resurrection**. Every believer who had died is raised from the dead at the same time: '... *and the dead in Christ will rise first'* (4:16b).

3. **There is a rapture**. Next comes the 'rapture' or 'ascent' of living Christians. We note that this being caught up is part of the one-and-only Second Coming of Jesus. *'Then we who are alive, those who are left, shall be caught up together with them in the clouds to meet the Lord in the air... '* (4:17b).

It is not that Jesus descends only part-way and then goes away again! When it says *'the Lord himself will descend from heaven'*, the descent is all of the way to the earth. When the Spirit *'descended'* on Jesus, the Spirit came all the way (Matthew 3:16; Mark 1:10; Luke 3:22; John 1:32, 33). When Jesus *'descended'* the first time as a baby in Bethlehem, He did not turn around half-way (John 3:13; 6:33, 38, 41, 42, 50, 51, 58). He is coming but we are caught up to meet him and come back with him.

4. **There is a reunion**. It is a day of wonderful meeting for all believers ever. Jesus comes all the way to earth with all of his people. There is no suggestion of a turn-around in the sky and it would require special mention if that is the way it would be.

The living Christians will be reunited with Jesus and with all who have been saved in the past ages. The 'meeting' does not mean that Jesus goes off with his people and does not come to earth! In Matthew 25:1 and 6 when five of the ten girls go out to 'meet' the bridegroom, the bridegroom does not turn around and go off with the ten girls! He keeps on coming and the girls accompany him. When in Acts

28:15–16 Paul was arriving in Rome, the Christians come out 'to meet' Paul, Paul does not collect them, turn around and go away. Rather the one arriving keeps on in the same direction, and the ones doing the meeting turn around and accompany their distinguished guest. This was the way the word 'meet' was generally used in this kind of situation. A visiting king or statesman would come, and the leading citizens would go out to meet him and would travel back with him. The visiting guest continues in the same direction.

That is the way it will be when Jesus comes. We meet him in the air. There is a glorious reunion of Jesus with all of his people. Then Jesus keeps on coming. He returns to earth and all of his people come with him.

5. **There is a result**. From that point on there will never be any separation from Jesus: '. . . *and so we shall for ever be with the Lord'*.

This teaching is to grip and encourage our hearts. To get a glimpse by faith of this one-and-only day when Jesus is revealed in His majesty and glory is wonderful. *'Therefore comfort one another with these words'* (4:18), says Paul. The comfort is that all believers, living or dead, will be reunited at Jesus' Second Coming. All will take part in the glorious events of those days. When Jesus comes, we shall come with him. When He is vindicated, we shall be vindicated. When the world recognizes him for who He is, they will recognize us for who we are. There can be nothing more encouraging.

This is the ultimate hope for the Christian. We are not just looking forward to death so as to be with Jesus. Death is never our hope! We are not simply looking forward to heaven. Heaven is not the ultimate hope, exactly. We are looking forward to the Day when Jesus will be utterly and wonderfully vindicated. Our hope is tied up with His hope! When He is finally and utterly glorified, the endless ages of eternal joy and service with Jesus will come for me and for all of God's redeemed people. Eternity has no end, and it will be eternity with Jesus and with the purified, happy, loving, joyful people of God.

Chapter 18

Living in the Overlap
(1 Thessalonians 5:1–6)

Paul's teaching about the Second Coming of Jesus began with the need to help distressed Christians whose loved ones had died (4:13–18). Now he widens the topic and looks at it more generally, considering the day of the Lord (5:1–3), and the call for watchfulness (5:4–8a).

When people consider the coming of God into human history they always want to know about dates and about periods of history – the *'times and the seasons'*. Paul had already given them teaching about this matter. *'Now concerning the times and the seasons, brothers and sisters, you do not have need to have anything written to you'* (5:1). He had evidently told them about seasons that would precede the coming of Jesus (perhaps mentioning both the period of the success of the gospel, and the period when it would face great opposition). Presumably he had already mentioned to them the suddenness and the unexpectedness of the final day. He does not feel that he needs to say much about these topics again. What he does in the following verses is not so much give fresh teaching, as urge them to readiness and watchfulness.

1. **He reminds them of the unexpectedness of Jesus' coming**. The Thessalonians wanted to know about times and seasons so as to be ready for Jesus to come. Paul reminds them that they already know that Jesus will come unexpectedly. He does not need to give them detailed teaching. *'For you*

yourselves know very well that the day of the Lord comes like a thief at night' (5:2). There are various terms for the Second Coming of Jesus. One of them is *'the day'*. We have reference to *'the day of the Lord'* (Acts 2:20; 2 Thessalonians 2:2; 2 Peter 3:10), *'the day of the Lord Jesus'* (1 Corinthians 5:5; 2 Corinthians 1:14), *'the day of our Lord Jesus Christ'* (1 Corinthians 1:8), *'the day of Jesus Christ'* (Philippians 1:6), *'the day of Christ'* (Philippians 1:10; 2:16), *'the day of God'* (2 Peter 3:12; Revelation 16:14), *'that day'* (Matthew 7:22; 14:36; 26:29; Luke 10:12; 2 Thessalonians 1:10; 2 Timothy 1:18), *'the last day'* (John 6:39, 40, 44, 45, 54; 11:24; 12:48), and *'his day'* (Luke 17:24). These expressions all refer to the one-and-only Second Coming of Jesus and the events that are closely connected with it at that time. (However there is a difference between *'the last day'* and *'the last days'*.)

The *'Day of the Lord'* is well-known as an Old Testament term, where it spoke of a future time when God would step in to judge His enemies and deliver His people. In the New Testament the phrase refers to the Second Coming of Jesus, and everything immediately connected with it. In 1 and 2 Thessalonians, Jesus' coming can also be called the *'coming'* (Greek: *parousia*; 1 Thessalonians 2:19; 3:13; 4:15; 5:23; 2 Thessalonians 2:1, 8), His *'coming down'* (1 Thessalonians 4:16), His *'revelation'* (*apokalypsis*; 2 Thessalonians 1:7) or His *'manifestation'* (*epiphaneia*; 2 Thessalonians 2:8). Every one of the four terms refers to the one-and-only Second Coming of Jesus.

The outstanding mark of the Second Coming is its suddenness and its unexpectedness. Anyone who has suffered at the hands of a burglar at night knows that it is a great shock. One knows in theory that it is possible yet the thief's robbery is nevertheless unexpected.

2. **The day of Jesus is a day when sin is abruptly destroyed**. The ungodly will get a great surprise in the day when God steps into the course of the world's history. *'When they say "peace and safety", then sudden destruction comes on them, as labour pains come on a pregnant woman, and they shall not escape'* (5:3). It will come unexpectedly, bringing a terrifying

intervention in all the wickedness of men and women. It will be like the labour pains of a woman in childbirth. Just as she knows they must come; so the sinner has a feeling in his heart that his sin will not go on indefinitely. Yet the first stab of pain still comes as a surprise.

At the time when Jesus comes people will be relaxed thinking that all is well and secure for them as they go on their wicked and God-defying ways. But just at a point where they feel so safe and secure in their sins, the end will come. Jesus will appear.

3. **The Christian lives in readiness for Jesus' coming**. Paul uses the word *'the day'* in another way. He is also using it to mean *'the daytime'*. *'But you, brothers and sisters, are not in darkness, in order that the day should surprise you as a thief does . . . '* (5:4). The coming of Jesus will bring the final kingdom of God. That age which is to come is like the daytime. The present age in which sin and wickedness are not extinguished is like night time. But the Christian is in the daytime already!

This is the common way in the New Testament of viewing the particular time of history that we are in. It can be put as a diagram like this:

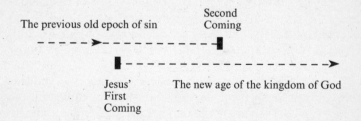

The previous old epoch of sin

Second Coming

Jesus' First Coming

The new age of the kingdom of God

The Christian is living in-between the First and Second Comings of Jesus. The kingdom of God has arrived; it arrived in Jesus. But the kingdom of sin is still here as well. At the moment sin has not been totally abolished. The Christian is living in an over-lap. Jesus' First Coming was the kingdom being initiated. Jesus' Second Coming will be the kingdom of sin being terminated. Meanwhile both are side-by-side, like wheat and weeds growing in one field (Matthew 13:24–43).

Paul says: *'for you are all children of light and children of the day. We are not of the night or of darkness'* (5:5). Christians know about the coming day of God. They will not be surprised by it. They know that they do not really belong to this present evil age. They belong to the kingdom of the future.

Then Paul says: *'So then let us not be asleep as others do, but let us stay awake and be sober'* (5:6). The argument is: be what you are! You are the people of God, says Paul. You belong to the coming daytime. So live accordingly.

Chapter 19

Clothes for the Daytime
(1 Thessalonians 5:7–8)

Paul is still working out his 'night and day' illustration. The kingdom of God is like the coming of the day – but it is here already! The sin of the world is like the gloom of night but it is dragging on. The coming day has not quite banished the gloom and darkness of the kingdom of sin.

1. **The night is used for sleep**. Paul is working out his illustration. The kingdom of sin which is still continuing in this world is like night-time. *'For those who sleep sleep at night, and those who are drunk get drunk at night'* (5:7). At night people sleep. Men and women of the world are unconscious of the things of God. They go on their ways foolishly, getting nearer and nearer to the coming of Jesus in judgement, quite unconscious of what their situation is.

2. **The night is used for drunkenness**. When sinners stay up late it is normally for the purposes of sin. People speak of the 'night life' of the great cities. That is exactly what it is! Night-time is used for wickedness because it is thought to give some kind of 'cover'. Perhaps people will not notice what is happening because it is dark! *'I saw the simple fools ... in the twilight, in the evening, at the time of night and darkness'* (Proverbs 7:9).

3. **People in the daytime are sober and awake**. Generally people are somewhat wiser in the daytime, and are more sober and wakeful. The Christian is a man or woman of the daytime. *'But since we belong to the day, let us be sober ...'*

71

(5:8). The Christian knows what he is doing. He is not avoiding sin simply as a matter of tradition or because his parents brought him up nicely! He knows who he is. He knows he belongs to the coming 'daytime' of the approaching kingdom of God. One day, maybe sooner than we think, Jesus is about to come. The night-time is on its way out already!

This is the Christian way of preaching holiness. It is not simply a matter of law or tradition. We know who we are. We are simply working out (Philippians 2:12) what is already true of us. It is natural for us to be wide-awake and sober in the things of God. We know who we are. We know the daytime is here; the night-time is almost gone. It is quite natural and logical for us to throw off the works of darkness.

4. **People in the daytime wear appropriate clothes**. People generally do not sleep in the clothes they wear during the day. Westerners wear pyjamas. In other parts of the world people might sleep with a night-cloth of some kind wrapped around them. But they do not sleep in the clothing that they used when they went to the office earlier in the day!

Men and women of the world belong to the old darkness. They wear the clothes of the dark – the clothing of their wicked ways. But Paul says to the Christians: *'since we belong to the day, let us be sober and put on the breastplate of faith and love, and the hope of salvation as a helmet'* (5:8). It is all very logical and appropriate. Since we belong to the day let us throw off the clothing of the old way of living and put on some clean clothes! And since we are soldiers in the army of Jesus, our clothing must include the clothing ready for battle and conflict. We have a breastplate and we have a helmet, like a Roman soldier.

The breastplate is 'faith and love'. The Christian life begins with faith but it works out as love. We begin by believing and we continue believing, again and again, in every situation. Then our faith in Jesus works out as love. Faith and love together make a breastplate. Nothing can throw us down and defeat us if we are walking in faith and love. They function as a kind of breastplate, a covering of the heart and chest which we need to stay alive.

The helmet is the hope of salvation. Roman officers used

to wear a helmet with large brightly coloured feathers. It made him proud to be a Roman. The Christian has something similar. There is something that makes him hold his head high. There is something that lets everyone know that he is an officer in the army of the king. It is *'the hope of salvation'*. Roman soldiers generally expected to win any battle they were in. They were rarely defeated. So they were proud to be unconquerable Romans! Their officers were proud of their brightly coloured helmets.

So it is with the Christian. Jesus is coming soon. The battle is about to finish altogether. Sin and Satan are about to be utterly defeated and exterminated. The final stage of the Christian's salvation is coming at any moment.

It is this sure and certain knowledge that we are about to be victorious that makes the Christian live in the way that he should. Christian holiness is not a matter of law. It is not for preachers to be endlessly bullying us and rebuking us and scolding us. The biblical way of holiness is to get us to see what is true about ourselves. We need some exhortation, but exhortations to holiness are just an appeal that we should see things aright, see them as they really are. The truth is that we are already God's people. Sin has already been defeated by the coming of Jesus. The night is far spent, the day is at hand. If we have any sense at all we shall see the reality of our situation and throw off the 'night-clothes' of the worldly way of living. We shall put on the armour for a short and sharp fight. It will soon be over, and we shall exchange the garments of battle for the garments of festivity and rejoicing!

Chapter 20

Finding Confidence in God

(1 Thessalonians 5:9–11)

Verses 9–10 of 1 Thessalonians 5 develop the point that Paul left us with at the end of verse 8. We are on our way to our final salvation. We can hold our heads high with the helmet of salvation, because our king is leading the battle and soon will appear Himself!

Let us put on the hope of salvation as a helmet, says Paul. *'For God has not destined us for wrath but for obtaining salvation through our Lord Jesus Christ* (5:9). *He has died for us so that whether we are awake or asleep we shall live together with him* (5:10). *Therefore give encouragement to one another and build up one another, just as you are doing'* (5:11).

Paul is developing further what it means to be wearing the *'helmet of salvation'*. It means amongst others things that we have a total confidence that we have already been accepted by God. When the final appearing of Jesus takes place there will be no wrath for those who have been persisting in faith and love.

1. **There is assurance for us because of the plan of God**. It is a mysterious subject and we must all be careful not to say more than we know. The Bible teaches that our salvation was rooted in God's choosing us. He has had a plan of salvation that has been working out since before the foundation of the world. It is that plan in which every Christian has a part. We were *'ordained to eternal life'* (Acts 13:49). It is a great mystery why God did it this way – but He did. The thought

74

that encourages the Christian is that God has never, ever, planned to pour out His wrath on the Christian. If we have a taste of wrath in judgement day (as Paul in Ephesians 5:6–7 suggests could happen) it will be because we have not been covered with faith and love. God's plan is that at the appearing of Jesus we shall receive the final phase of salvation. Only the rebellious will *'shrink in shame at his coming'* (1 John 2:28) and be *'saved through fire'* (1 Corinthians 3:15). The Christian does not need to fear eternal hell at all! And he need not fear the judgement day – as long as he persists in faith and love.

Salvation has stages in it. First comes our justification – our being clothed with the righteousness of Jesus. Then comes what is called *'working out our salvation'* (Philippians 2:12). God is at work in us (Philippians 2:13) and we co-operate with Him in living a godly life. We are being progressively rescued or 'saved' from the damage that sin has done to us in our past lives and through the sinfulness which we inherited.

Then there is a third stage of salvation, and this is what we are waiting for, and what Paul is speaking of here. Sin is to be removed from the personality altogether. New bodies are to be given to us. Everything we have done for Jesus and His kingdom is somehow to be given back to us, and Jesus is to say 'Well done' to us. This is what we are destined for! When Jesus comes the last stage will be brought into effect. Let us put on the hope of salvation as a helmet, says Paul. *'For God has not destined us for wrath but for obtaining salvation through our Lord Jesus Christ'* (5:9).

2. **There is an assurance that comes to us through the blood of Jesus Christ**. Paul knows that we shall be somewhat afraid of the judgement day. The knowledge that we have been destined for salvation should help us, but there is more! *'He has died for us so that whether we are awake or asleep we shall live together with him'* (5:10). In case we have any fears, Paul reminds us of the blood of Jesus Christ. Our sins have been paid for. We need not fear that we shall be cast into hell to be left there for ever or to be exterminated in some way. The blood of Jesus Christ has paid the price for our sins. The

blood of Jesus Christ is the deepest and the ultimate ground of our feeling safe. We cannot rest on the quality of our faith or the quality of our love. We all know what it is to have the *'breastplate of faith and love'* slip for a while – and maybe for more than a while! The ultimate resting place for our faith is the blood of Jesus. He died for us!

> I need no other argument,
> I need no other plea;
> It is enough that Jesus died,
> And that He died for me.

And it makes no difference whether I am dead or alive at the time of Jesus' coming. *'Whether **awake** (that is, we have not yet died) or **asleep** (that is, we have died), we shall live together with him'*. The Thessalonians were worried about those who had died. Paul says, 'Don't worry about it!' Those who have died shall be raised first. Those who are still alive shall be transformed and shall join the raised-from-the-dead believers. The ground of our certainty and confidence is that we are united with Jesus. *'We shall live together with him'*. We do not get to glory because of how good we are. We get to the final salvation because we are united to Jesus Christ and nothing can separate us from Him.

3. **There is an assurance that comes to us through each other**. Paul can tell them to be bold and confident and encouraged. *'Therefore give encouragement to one another and build up one another, just as you are doing'* (5:11).

We take courage ourselves, and we get others to rejoice also. His words are a classic illustration of the way in which Christian truth encourages and builds us up. The truth sets us free!

Chapter 21

Staying Together in Jesus
(1 Thessalonians 5:12–15)

Paul is getting towards the end of his letter. He approaches his conclusion by giving his Thessalonian friends a string of short and sharp words of exhortation. There are sixteen of them in verses 12–22. The exhortations get shorter as they go along.

1. The first is: **respect your leaders**. Christian leaders are to be followed. *'Now we are asking you, brothers and sisters, to acknowledge those who are working among you and are leading you in the Lord and who instruct you'* (5:12)

The church is not a one-man-one-vote democracy, and westerners especially need to be careful that they do not bring one-man-one-vote ideas into the Christian church. It is fine for the state – if a high enough consensus exists in the nation. But the church has leaders who are to be voluntarily given respect simply because they are put where they are by God. (Civic leaders get a certain amount of respect for the same reason – Romans 13:2.) So Paul says: acknowledge those who ... instruct you, *'and esteem them very highly in love because of their work'* (5:13a). It must be remembered that some of these leaders might be foreigners. Possibly some Jewish leaders were in the church. Paul himself was Jewish. Silvanus was Jewish; Timothy was half-Jewish. Yet all the leaders were to be shown love and respect.

Of course if a Christian leader sins badly or commands that we should sin, we should *'obey God rather than any human authority'* (Acts 5:29), but in other respects the leaders of the fellowship should be given respect, loyalty and, as much as possible, obedience.

Paul's words also have a few hints for the leaders themselves. They are to lead! They have a responsibility to get to a knowledge of God's will and lead the people in it. They are to instruct the people. The word of God must be applied in the lives of the Thessalonian Christians.

2. Next: *'Be at peace among yourselves'* (5:13b). Christian congregations reach every kind of person, every temperament, every section of society. So it is specially necessary for churches to keep an eye on the harmony of the congregation. Paul addresses the entire congregation. The peace of Christ must rule among them (Colossians 3:15).

3. *'And we urge you, brothers and sisters, instruct the unruly'* (5:14a).

We have noticed before that there was a group in Thessalonica who liked the excitement of the teaching about the Second Coming of Jesus, but they did not like practical discipline. They tended to make dogmatic predictions, and were in danger of neglecting quite ordinary things. They preferred to get what they called 'a ministry' (if their modern successors are anything to judge by) and wanted to meddle in other peoples' lives rather than get on with their 'ordinary' responsibilities.

Paul says they must be instructed. The leaders must take steps to help such people.

4. *'Encourage the people who are fearful'* (5:14b). There was much in the Thessalonian situation that was alarming. The Christians were facing a lot of opposition. Some had died and then the idea got around that they would miss the blessings of Jesus' final kingdom, So Paul says: encourage the fearful. Christians need help. The Christian life does not go ahead with its own power as if we needed no help from outside. We ought not to need help. We have everything provided that pertains to life and godliness. But in point of fact, Christians need help from pastors and leaders.

5. *'Help the weak'* (5:14c). There would be people who needed to be specially supported. Some would be weak in

faith, needlessly legalistic and unnecessarily hard on them-selves. People who are highly legalistic are not called 'strong' or 'holy'. Legalism is not strength; it is weakness! In New Testament times there were people who were ultra-strict about being vegetarian or about the keeping of special days. No doubt Thessalonica had its own cultural legalisms. Paul calls it *'weakness'* (see Romans 14; 1 Corinthians 8–10) and says such people need help.

6. *'Be patient with everyone'* (5:14d). There are always a great deal of spiritual problems in the lives of any large group of people. The danger for the leaders of the Thes-salonian Christians was that they would become discouraged and begin to be impatient with those who were slow to learn or who had problems of temperament. Christian mutual encouragement takes patience.

7. **Refuse vindictiveness** (5:15). Paul says *'see that no one repays evil with evil . . . '* (5:15a). It is very natural to the human race to be vindictive. Every man or woman has an inner desire to 'get his own back' in one way or another. It might be in actions; it might be in words. But justice has to be left to God. God likes to have the matter of justice in His own hands. Nothing tests the quality of our resting in the sovereignty of God more than this. Are we willing to leave our case and our cause in the hands of God? Are we willing to refuse any kind of vindictiveness or self-seeking? Paul, like Jesus, asks that we be positively out-going in love to the one who has harmed us. In Thessalonica there were people who had persecuted the Christians. Bitterness and resentment towards them would have been understandable. But Paul says: refuse to be bitter!

8. Positively, they are to be people of goodwill: *'. . . but always seek to do that which is good for one another and for everyone'* (5:15b). Love has to be shown to the fellowship in Thessalonica. And love has to be shown towards the out-siders, some of whom are violently opposing the Christians. Even the worst person is made in the image of God. He or she might yet be saved. Our enemies might yet become our friends. If we follow the pathway of love, who knows what blessing might pour down upon us?

Chapter 22

Rejoicing at All Times

(1 Thessalonians 5:16–18)

Paul's practical exhortations continue.

9. *'Rejoice at all times'* (5:16). It was a challenging call to the Thessalonians since they were enduring many hardships. Yet they were already living a life of joy amidst hardship. They had *'received the word, amidst affliction, with the joy of the Holy Spirit'* (1:6). Paul speaks too of the joy he finds in ministry to the Thessalonians. *'What is our ... joy ...? Is it not you? For you are our joy'* (2:19–20). *'What thanks can we give for the joy that we have because of you ... ?'* (3:9). These passing references make it clear that for Paul, joy is joy in God, joy in serving God, joy in God's people.

Now he asks them to go on rejoicing. The fact that Paul makes it an exhortation shows that rejoicing has a lot to do with attitude. It is not joy in pleasant circumstances, because the Thessalonians were not in pleasant circumstances. They had endured persecution and were likely to endure yet more. But Paul still calls them to rejoice.

It is a matter of attitude. It begins when we refuse grumpiness or aggressiveness or resentment. It comes when we take ourselves in hand, as the Psalmist did. We talk to ourselves! *'Why are you cast down, O my soul?'* (Psalm 42:5). We give ourselves the reasons for rejoicing in God. We remind ourselves of our relationship to God, and our security. We point ourselves to God's faithfulness, and the way in which He has not abandoned us. *'Hope in God! For I shall yet praise*

him, my help and my God!' (Psalm 42:5). Paul urges us to
do it.

We must rejoice at all times! Learn to leave your case and
your cause in the hands of God. Set your hearts and minds
on God's goodness and faithfulness. He does not disappoint
us. Make a practice of Christian love no matter what is
happening to you. Only a person of love can be a person of
joy. No one can rejoice while he is feeling guilty, so keep a
clear conscience, keep trusting the blood of Jesus, and
rejoice!

10. *'Pray constantly'* (5:17). Paul has spoken of his own
constancy in prayer (1:2–3), and he has given us some hints
as to the topics of his praying. As well as expressing his gratitude, he prays for the Christians that he is responsible for
(1:2–3), and he lets them know that he makes the work in
Thessalonica a matter of prayer. *'Night and day we pray very
intensely that we may see you . . . '* (3:10). He asks God that his
way to them might be prospered. And he prays for their
growth in spirituality (3:9–13; 5:23–24).

Now he asks them to follow his example. *'Pray constantly!'*
It does not mean that one is literally praying under ones's
breath all the time, and living an ultra-religious life. That
kind of life soon becomes a bondage and a hypocrisy.

Also he is not saying that we can have an 'attitude of
prayer' without actually praying, but really be praying all
the time. That also soon becomes rather hypocritical. If we
find a way of praying that is not really praying, we shall
neglect actual praying!

The command surely implies that (i) we persistently have
times when we turn aside from other things in order to pray,
and (ii) that we get into the habit – without being a religious
nuisance to others – of constantly turning to God for help
and guidance, at all times of the day or night.

How important it is to pray! The greatest example is Jesus.
Prayer was obviously the habit of His life. He was praying at
His baptism (Luke 3:21, 22). He would sometimes withdraw
to pray. *'He departed and went into a lonely place'* for prayer
(Luke 4:42; see also Mark 1:35). Sometimes when He was at
the height of His popularity and one would expect to find

Him enjoying the fame, we discover that He would withdraw and find time to pray (Luke 5:15–16).

Jesus is the best interpreter. He was a man who *'prayed constantly'*.

11. *'Be grateful'*. One can see why a call for gratitude should follow on a call for prayer. Thanksgiving is one part of prayer, and the request-type of praying should always be mixed with thanksgiving. Paul often puts the two side-by-side. *'We ... give thanks ... and mention you in our prayers...'* (1:2–3). He tells people how grateful he is to God. *'We also thank God constantly for this...'* (2:13). Now he asks them to be grateful just as he is endlessly grateful to God. The circumstances of the Thessalonians might tempt them to ingratitude, but they must not let their hardships damage their spirit. *'Give thanks in all circumstances, for this is God's will in Christ Jesus for you'* (5:18).

Sometimes in the midst of adversity it is good to turn aside and deliberately go over the many things for which we must thank God: the story of our lives in which we have experienced many mercies and wonderful leadings. The way in which He has given us life and (for most of us) health and strength. The way in which He led us to Himself and we discovered Jesus to be a Saviour. The leadings and the outpourings of His Holy Spirit. The many blessings we have received (most of us) in work, in our families and among our friends. The joy we have in His kingdom and in the ministry we have in His church (in one way or another). And then there are the blessings of His kingdom. *'All spiritual blessings!'* Paul calls them (Ephesians 1:3). The list is endless.

This is God's will in Christ Jesus for you. It may not always be your will, but it is God's will, and there are times when God's will has to be deliberately followed and our will has to be deliberately left aside. Daily, regularly, constantly, thanking God is God's will for your life and mine.

Chapter 23

Living in the Spirit

(1 Thessalonians 5:19–22)

The following words of command deal with openness to the Holy Spirit coupled with care about what claims to be from the Spirit.

12. *'Do not extinguish the Spirit'* (5:19). There was obviously a lot of spiritual power in the church at Thessalonica. Paul himself had preached *'not ... in word only but ... in power and in the Holy Spirit and with much conviction'*. Clearly that spiritual power had continued with them. It was like a fire. Paul urges them not to resist this power of the Spirit. It is possible to *'put out the fire'*, and Paul warns them not to let it happen.

The desire to dampen the Spirit's voice may come when the Spirit is becoming demanding with regard to repentance, when He is introducing new directions into the life of the church, when the Spirit's power is causing criticism among unbelievers, or when the spirit of ill-will arises because of bitterness or criticism. Paul says: don't let it happen. Do not extinguish the fire of the Holy Spirit.

13. *'Do not despise prophesying ... '* (5:20). To 'prophesy' is a word with a wide range of meaning. It is obvious that there are various levels of prophecy. Sometimes a prophecy might come which is verbally inspired – as the Old Testament prophets spoke with words put into their mouths (see Jeremiah 1:9). But often prophecy operates at a much lower

level than this! Sometimes it is simply that the man or woman has some kind of revelation from God – but it is by no means verbally inspired. Sometimes there may be some error mixed in with truth, as when Agabus seems to have been almost but not entirely right in his prediction which he gave to Paul in Acts 21:10–11. Paul was not bound by the Jews but by the Romans (21:33; 22:29). The Jews did not deliver him to the Romans but tried to kill Paul (21:31) and the Romans had to rescue him.

There are various levels of prophecy. The danger is that because of the difficulties (error, eccentricity, bizarre behaviour in the speakers, and so on) we altogether dismiss the whole matter of God's speaking to us through another. Paul says: be ready for God to speak to you through another person.

14. '... *but test everything*' (5:21). Prophecies should not simply be accepted. Paul disregarded Agabus' prophecy. It is obvious that he did not just accept everything that was said to him.

How should prophecy be tested? By previous revelations. God will not contradict what He has already said, especially within Scripture. 'New doctrines' that come through prophecy should be rejected. Non-fulfillment of predictions should be noted (although predictions are sometimes fulfilled in unexpected ways). Any 'prophesying' which seems to get the 'prophet' a lot of money is suspect. The general impact that the speaker has should be noted. Does it lead into spirituality, into zeal for Christian love, into balanced personality? Not all of this can be instantly seen. Sometimes *'testing everything'* takes time. Above all the Christians must be willing to think, to consider, and then to speak and act. Some are too 'soft' and although doubts about someone's 'prophecies' grow, they fear speaking out. Some are too 'hard' and scarcely anything new or surprising is allowed to pass the test.

Sometimes a word from God through another person is warm, encouraging, obviously in harmony with Scripture. The greatest prophecies of all are prophetic exposition of Scripture where the prophecy has a firmly biblical base and yet it has appropriateness and is very immediate and contemporary. Then we know we are hearing from God.

15. *'Hold fast what is good'* (5:21). When fresh revelation is coming from God we have to be careful to retain what is good. This is true in a number of ways. There may be a mixture of what is good and what is false. Agabus' prediction obviously had some 'good' in it. It prepared Paul to face coming danger. Paul went to Jerusalem ready to die, if need be, for the sake of the gospel (Acts 21:13). Agabus' prediction perhaps roused him to added readiness to face anything that might be ahead of him. Yet not everything Agabus said was 100% accurate.

There is another sense in which we have to *'hold fast what is good'*, and that is that we have to retain the things that God has taught us in days gone by as He gives us further understanding of His will and His ways. God will reveal new things to us (see Philippians 3:16), but *'let us hold true to what we have attained'* (Philippians 3:16). If we get over-excited about new revelations we are likely to become somewhat unbalanced. New words from God have to take their place in the entire landscape of what God has said. If we make a part to be the whole, we shall have imbalance.

16. *'Avoid evil in every form'* (5:21b). The King James or Authorised Version is somewhat misleading in its translation, when it speaks of every *'appearance'* of evil. It seems to be telling us not to give a bad impression. That is quite acceptable teaching (see Romans 14:16) but it is not what Paul is saying. He is not saying 'Abstain from what **appears** to be evil – but maybe it is not evil at all!' Rather he is saying 'Abstain from anything that **is** evil, in any form in which it may take'. Under the leading of the Holy Spirit the Thessalonians will come across things that are evil. They will discover that the deceits of the devil are varied. They might be tempted to reject evil in one way but accept it in another. Paul says: when God has shown you something is wrong reject it! Even if it comes through an angel of light, reject it. Avoid evil in every form in which it comes to you, even when it comes through the greatest speaker, or the greatest claims

to inspiration. Let God lead you and guide you, says Paul, and then act on what He says. Hold fast what is good. Avoid evil in every form.

Chapter 24

'God is Faithful...'
(1 Thessalonians 5:23–28)

Paul now brings his letter to a close as he prays for the Thessalonians (5:23–24), requests prayer for himself (5:25), and in a friendly way ends his letter (5:26–28).

1. **First, he prays for the Thessalonians' complete sanctification**. 1 Thessalonians 5:23 is a famous verse in connection with teaching about 'body, soul and spirit'. *'Now may the God of peace himself sanctify you completely; and may your whole spirit, soul and body be kept blameless for the coming of our Lord Jesus Christ'* (5:23).

Paul thinks of God as *'the God of peace'* – the God who wants all disunity among His people and all division within ourselves to come to an end; the God who wants us to have a totally happy conscience. He prays that we might be sanctified *'completely'*. This does not mean with a measure of holiness so that we do not need to confess sin; or such that we do not need to pray *'Forgive us our trespasses'*. It is not that he expects us in this life to be as sinless as Jesus. No kind of perfection like that was imagined by Paul in this life.

The next line explains what he means by being *'sanctified wholly'*. It is that every aspect of our life is affected by the cleansing of God. Our bodies are put at God's disposal. Our souls – our inner lives – are straightforward, honest, pure, clean. Our spirits – our relationship to God – is believing, optimistic, full of assurance of God's grace. It is not that we are as sinless as Jesus, but it is surely possible to have every aspect of our life basically right, basically honest.

However the verse is often somewhat misused as though it were talking about three 'pieces' of the human personality. Yet 'soul' and 'spirit' are sometimes interchangeable terms. *'My soul praises the Lord'* in Luke 1:46 has the same meaning as *'My spirit rejoices in God'* in the next line. It is a mistake to regard 'body', 'soul' and 'spirit' as **parts** of the human nature. Rather, they are **aspects**. My body is my physical frame. In a rare verse like this one where subtle distinctions are being made, my soul is my inner life, my feelings, my emotions, my conscience. My spirit is not another 'part' of me but that same inner life in its orientation to God.

It is quite possible to view the human personality as having many angles. Mark 12:30 talks of four (heart, soul, mind and strength). 1 Thessalonians adds two more (spirit, body). One could add a few more still, notably 'conscience'. One must not deduce how many 'bits' there are in man by how many words one can find like this.

Paul is praying that every aspect of the Thessalonians' personality may be pure and clean. He makes it a matter of prayer. That suggests that the Thessalonians also ought to make it a matter of prayer and genuine exertion. To be straight with God! To have a good conscience in every department of life! This is Paul's wish for them.

He prays that they might be this way 'for' the coming of our Lord Jesus Christ. The translation is surely not 'at' the coming. We shall certainly be sanctified 'at' the coming. We do not need to pray about that! The sense is *'so as to be blameless in the coming . . . '*. It is simplest to translate it, 'for' the coming. Paul's language, as often, is compressed.

2. **He has confidence that his prayer will be answered**. He wants some kind of total uprightness and integrity in the Thessalonians, and he is convinced that God can do it. It is God's will to do it at the Second Coming. Of course we shall be perfect in body and soul in the day of the resurrection. That can be taken for granted; we do not even have to pray about it. Paul is thinking of something that we do have to pray for, and that he is wanting to take place in this life. He

is looking for an all-round integrity in the life of the Thessalonians, a life ready to be presented to God at the time of the Second Coming. It is this he is thinking of when he adds: *'The one who calls you is faithful and He will do it'* (5:24). We can pray that we get to this kind of all-round integrity. We might be aware of weakness and imperfection, and yet at the same time we might also be conscious of honesty and integrity. Paul could say *'We have conducted ourselves ... in holiness and sincerity ... not according to worldly wisdom but according to God's grace'* (2 Corinthians 1:12). He is not claiming absolutely sinlessness, but he is claiming all-round integrity. The one who calls you is faithful and He will do it.

3. **Paul asks them to pray for him also**. He is not so spiritually superior as to think that only they need prayer. He needs prayer also and he knows it. *'Brothers and sisters pray for us'* (5:25).

He asks that his love to the fellowship should be expressed among themselves. *'Greet all the brothers and sisters with a holy kiss'* (5:26). He insists with great authority that his letter should be publicly read, as the Old Testament scriptures would be publicly read. *'I require you by the Lord that this letter be read to all the brothers and sisters'* (5:27). And he closes with his prayer that God's grace will be with them: *'The grace of our Lord Jesus Christ be with you'* (5:28). Throughout his closing words one can feel what is on his heart. He wants the Thessalonian fellowship to be a place of ease, of openly expressed affection, of happy submission to Paul's apostolic authority. He knows that by the grace of God such a life in such a church is possible. The one who calls is faithful and He will do it.

Chapter 25

Rooted in Faith and Love

(2 Thessalonians 1:1–4)

'2 Thessalonians' as its name suggests was the second letter
to be sent to the church at Thessalonica. One gets the impression in 1 Thessalonians that the Christians had recently come
to salvation, but in 2 Thessalonians one gets the impression
that various developments have gone a stage further. 2 Thessalonians 2:15 refers to a previous letter. So it is likely that
'2 Thessalonians' was written not long after 1 Thessalonians.

Paul is still in Corinth and still with Silas and Timothy.
The gospel has spread further than Thessalonica. Persecution
has got worse. The teaching concerning the Second Coming
was being misunderstood and matters were made worse
because of a false letter that had reached the Thessalonians
(2 Thessalonians 2:2). The 'disorderly' or 'unruly' people
were as much a problem as ever. Paul writes to give them the
positive teaching that is needed by the different sections of
the fellowship.

1. **First, we have a description of the church** (1:1). He
announces himself as the author, and as having the support
of his two co-workers. *'Paul, Silvanus and Timothy, to the
church of the Thessalonians in God our Father and the Lord
Jesus Christ'* (1:1). Once again (as in 1 Thessalonians 1:1) he
calls them the church *'in God'*. The church is a body of people
'in' God the Father and *'in Jesus Christ'*. The people of God
are *'in'* Him. That is, they are joined on to Him. They get
their life and energy from Him. He guides them, empowers

them, provides for them. Thessalonica was a difficult place for Christians. But they are not only in Thessalonica. They are in God, in Jesus.

2. Next, we have **a description of what they need** (1:2). Paul gives his opening word of greeting. *'Grace to you and peace from God the Father and the Lord Jesus Christ'* (1:2). They need God's grace and peace – in that order. It is God's graciousness to us that leads to the peace of God in our lives.

3. Again, as in nearly all his letters, **his gratitude to God is expressed early in his letter**.

He was grateful for their growing faith in God. He has noticed that their faith is growing and he is so grateful for that. In 1 Thessalonians he mentioned their faith (1 Thessalonians 1:3); here he takes note that it is growing. *'We are obliged always to give thanks to God for you, brothers and sisters, as is proper, because your faith is growing abundantly . . .'* (1:3a).

Everything that lives grows. Plants, trees, animals, babies – beings that have life in them generally grow. When a pastor sees new Christians growing in faith he knows that they are truly saved and have the life of God within them.

Faith is growing when it is able to stand ever stronger against trials and troubles; when we panic less, and maintain our peace and calmness more. The Thessalonians were facing a lot of opposition, but Paul feels confident about them. He can see that their faith is growing stronger amidst the opposition that is coming against them.

Faith is growing when we are able to accept greater challenges. At one stage in our lives we are not so able to do great things for God. The things that great men and women of faith have done before seem to be too great for us to do! But then we start doing something for God and we discover that God is with us! Eventually we are able to do greater things for God than we ever did before. Our faith is growing by sheer experience of God's power and goodness. The people that know God are able to do greater things for Him than they could in the earlier days of their life. They are able to stand amidst greater trials. They continue believing despite delay and despite their own weaknesses.

Is my faith growing? Is yours? Are we able to stand against greater troubles? Do we have greater vision than ever for the kingdom of God? Are we more determined than ever to live a godly life by faith in the power of God's Holy Spirit? Is my vision of what I can do for God growing?

Paul was grateful for their growing love towards each other. The Christian life begins with faith but ends in love. Paul says: *'We are obliged always to give thanks to God for you ... because your faith is growing ...* **and the love of every one of you for the others is increasing'** (1:3). All of the resources of the Christian life begin with faith. Faith is the starting point of every blessing. But the end product is love. This world is a fallen and wicked world. There is so much hostility around. Within families, within clans and tribes, within churches sometimes – everywhere – the world has a lot of hatred in it. But amidst a world of hatred, Paul is grateful to see a people who are growing in love. It is a miracle. Only the grace of God can do it. Only faith in our Lord Jesus Christ can produce love amidst a world like this one. Paul sees the love of the Christians at Thessalonica getting greater and greater, and he thinks it wonderful. So should we. It should be our greatest aim: to be a people of growing love.

Paul was grateful for their endurance amidst hardships. Faith and love make us strong. Paul could see how strong in Jesus these Thessalonians were becoming, and he used their example to encourage other churches. *'So among God's churches we ourselves boast about you. We boast about your perseverance and the faithfulness amidst all the persecutions and afflictions you are enduring'* (1:4). When people have growing faith and growing love, it gives them great strength. God is pleased with them. The fellowship holds together. They have a happy spirit. These Thessalonians were enduring great trials and standing firm because they were rooted in faith and in love.

Chapter 26

A Day for Repayment

(2 Thessalonians 1:5–8)

Paul has introduced himself and his readers (1:1–2) and has given his thanksgiving for the Thessalonians' faith, love and perseverance (1:3–4). Now he turns to his first main subject which, once again, is the Second Coming of Jesus Christ.

The main idea of verses 5–12 is that when Jesus comes again it will be a day when all injustices are rectified, and people receive back from God judgements and rewards according to the way they have treated the people of God.

There is to be a judgement of works. It will not be a judgement about faith but a judgement of what we have done and the way we have treated other people. Every person in the world will give account to God of the way in which he or she has lived and the deeds that he or she has done, good and bad. Although no Christian need fear being thrown to eternal hell, even Paul can speak of the *'terror of the Lord'* (2 Corinthians 5:11) because of the seriousness of the judgement of works.

The Thessalonians are obviously suffering greatly. There are people in Thessalonica who are deliberately *'afflicting'* them (as 1:6 says). Paul points them to the fact that justice is on its way, more thorough and just than anyone can imagine.

Paul has just referred to the great endurance of the Christians. Now he goes on: *'This is an indication[1] of the righteous decision of God. His purpose is[2] that you should be counted worthy of the kingdom of God, on behalf of which you are now suffering'* (1:5). God has a made a righteous decision about trials and troubles.

1. **God has decided that progress in the kingdom of God should come through afflictions and adversities**. His plan is that He should bring us into ever deeper experience of the blessings of His kingdom by using trouble in our lives.

It is often thought that *'the kingdom of God'* in this verse is the final kingdom after Jesus comes, but I doubt it. It is a regular part of Paul's teaching and New Testament teaching that we inherit the blessings of the kingdom now in this life. It is a kingdom of righteousness, peace and joy in the Holy Spirit – even now! By means of many tribulations we inherit the kingdom (see Acts 14:22) – even now. We count it joy to endure tribulations because we know that in this life God is making us more accessible to His training in our lives.

When we suffer troubles *'for the sake of the name'* (Acts 5:41), it does something for us. It modifies our character, toughens up our endurance, separates us somewhat from our pride, and intensifies our experience of the Spirit (as 1 Peter 4:14 says). We are being *'counted worthy'* of reward, the reward of a deeper experience of the kingdom of God in our lives.

2. **God has decided that the afflictions of His people will eventually be avenged**. His plan is that the sufferings His people endure should assist them in the kingdom of God, but then the tormenters should be justly punished.

'It is a righteous decision, since it is a just thing with God to repay with affliction the ones afflicting you...' (1:6). Eventually strict justice is dispensed. Persecutors receive back in their own experience the very things that have handed out to others. It is a common biblical theme. Men and women eventually receive back the due penalty of what they have done. It may take time, but justice is on its way.

On the other hand, God's people will eventually be rewarded not only with an experience of the kingdom in the here-and-now, but with something even greater. Paul continues: *'... and to repay you, the ones being afflicted, rest along with us, at the revelation of the Lord Jesus Christ from heaven with his powerful angels'* (1:7). The idea that *'entering rest'* is a reward is familiar from the letter to the Hebrews, but in Hebrews *'entering into rest'* is an experience in this life. It is what happens when God swears in His mercy to bless us. Actually the thought of receiving rest is used in three ways. (i) Matthew 11:28 refers to a rest that is found when we first come to Jesus. (ii) Matthew 11:29 and the letter to the Hebrews refer to an entering into rest that comes by taking Jesus' yoke and by persisting in faith. (iii) 2 Thessalonians 1:7 and Revelation 14:13 refer to an eternal rest. Hell is the experience of never resting (see Revelation 14:11). One could say that when Jesus comes, all believers will have for the last time the experience of *'entering into rest'*.

Paul adds another sentence describing the punishment of the lost: *'with flames of fire He will impose justice on those who do not know God, and do not obey the gospel of our Lord Jesus'* (1:8). The fire is the fire of God's holiness. It is the same fire that shone in the burning bush, against which Moses was warned since it was holy ground (Exodus 3:5). It is the same fire into which the unsaved are finally thrown (*'Depart . . . into everlasting fire . . .'*, Matthew 25:41).

There is only refuge, says Paul, for those who do know God and who obey the gospel. He leaves the way open. *'Those who know God'* is not a closed community. The offer of Jesus as Saviour is available for everyone. Those who were the Thessalonians' persecutors may yet be the Thessalonians' companions in trusting Jesus.

Footnotes

[1] The opening words are often translated 'This is evidence of the righteous judgement of God . . .' but it is difficult to make sense of that. How does enduring in suffering (1:4) prove or give evidence of God's righteous judgement? The meaning of the noun is not 'evidence' but (as suggested by the related verb) 'showing forth' or 'indication'. Compare New Jerusalem Bible: 'It all shows that . . .'.

[2] The Greek *eis* denotes the purpose of God's righteous decision. It is best to make it clear by starting a new sentence.

Chapter 27

Everlasting Destruction
(2 Thessalonians 1:9–12)

Paul develops his point that exact justice falls upon persecutors at the time of Jesus' coming. *'They will pay the penalty of eternal destruction so as to be separated from the presence of the Lord, separated from the glory of his might . . . '* (1:9).

1. **God's judgement has steps and stages in it**. Hell has a sequence of events. It is not simply a matter of being annihilated at death; and it is not a matter of there being a single one-off event of being thrown into hell. It is quite clear that there are stages in God's eternal punishment.

At one point during the 'judgement day' – which is not to be thought of as a 24–hour period – sinners will have to 'repay' what they have done. Quite what this involves is not known, but it will take time.

At some point the persecutor will, according to Revelation, be *'tormented with fire . . . in the presence of the Lamb'* (Revelation 14:10), but the sinner does not stay *'in the presence of the Lamb'* forever. Another stage is the penalty of *'eternal destruction'* from the presence of the Lord.

The word 'destruction' here is not the normal Greek word but a rarer word (*olethros*) which comes only four times in the New Testament (1 Corinthians 5:5; 1 Thessalonians 5:3; 2 Thessalonians 1:9; 1 Timothy 6:9) and has varied meanings. It occurs about twenty times in the Greek Old Testament, where it can refer to physical death (Wisdom 18:13; 2 Maccabees 13:6; 3 Maccabees 6:34) or the ruination that precedes removal (*'its destruction and its removal from the face of the earth'*, 1 Kings 13:34); disaster in battle (Judith 11:15), or the 'ruination' of metal objects (Hosea 9:6, Greek), of a city (Obadiah 13, Greek) or a country (Jeremiah 38:55; 31:3; Ezekiel 6:14; 14:16 – all in the Greek text; not our standard Hebrew or English texts). It is used of 'ruination' of crops (Jeremiah 31:32, Greek) especially in a time of war (3 Maccabees 6:30).

Important for understanding our verse are references to punishment. *'Destruction shall lodge with the ungodly'* says the Greek text of Proverbs 21:7. Earthly calamities *'punish the wicked to destruction'* says Sirach 39:30. *'Destruction'* is the disaster brought by sin that ruins a man's life (Proverbs 1:26, 27, Greek text).

Sometimes extermination is in view as when the 'death' is the opposite of 'immortality' and destruction consists of being *'consumed to nought'* (Wisdom 1:15). In the Greek text of Jeremiah 31:8 it is identified with being *'completely destroyed'* (*exolethreuthesetai*). It can refer to total extermination as opposed to limited destruction (*'not destruction . . . but chastening'*, 2 Maccabees 6:12). When the phrase *'eternal punishment of the tyrant'* (*ton aionion tou tyrannou olethron*) is used in 4 Maccabees 10:15, it means not a punishment that goes on for ever, but a punishment that is once-and-for-ever and never will be reversed. (I quote books outside the Old Testament not because they are Scripture but because they provide linguistic evidence.)

It is clear that 'destruction' is a very extreme measure that is one part of what is meant by hell. It eventually removes the persecutor from the presence of God and does so eternally.

It is also a matter of being *'separated from the glory of his might'*. The saved have the privilege of seeing God's glorious power, and of experiencing it in their own persons (*'raised in glory . . . raised in power'*, 1 Corinthians 15:43). The persecutors will be separated from such a privilege for ever.

2. **God's judgement commences at the Second Coming of Jesus**. Such a punishment for the persecutor begins, *'. . . whenever he comes to be glorified in his holy people and to*

97

be admired in all the ones who have believed – because our testimony to you was believed' (1:10).

At the time of Jesus' coming the persecutors will have their sins exposed, but God's people will have their righteousness exposed. After the persecutors have been consigned to condemnation God's people will rejoice in each other. Everyone will admire the righteousness produced in Jesus' people. The people of God will admire each other. The angels will marvel. Jesus will rejoice at seeing His own righteousness in His people.

It all takes place because of people who believed. Faith in the apostolic testimony was the beginning. Rejoicing in glory is the outcome.

3. **Paul's teaching about the Second Coming should motivate us to prayer and zeal**. Paul's words about the Second Coming certainly motivate him. He turns immediately to prayer for the Thessalonians. *'To this end also we are praying always for you, in order that our God may make you worthy of his call . . . '*. He knows that they have been 'called' to salvation and to high levels of glory in the last day. Now he prays that in their life they may become worthy of the reward that God wants to give them. It has nothing to do with deserving salvation. It has everything to do with living in such a way that God rewards us at the end. He prays that God may make them worthy *' . . . and may fulfill by his power every good resolve and work of faith . . . '* (1:11). There has to be a determination to 'follow through' in the Christian life. God gives purposes in our hearts, and we can see that there are works of faith to be done. Paul turns these matters into prayer and asks God that the resolve may be supported by God's power and so may be achieved.

The aim of everything is honour being brought to Jesus. *'We ask this so that the name of our Lord Jesus may be glorified in you, and you in him, according to the grace of our God and the Lord Jesus Christ'*.

The final goal of everything is the honour of Jesus through us, but also honour comes to us through Jesus. Jesus shares His glory. Through God's grace Paul is expecting it to happen in the lives of these Thessalonian Christians who not long ago were pagans living in a city that had heard nothing of Jesus at all. When God is at work progress may be swift.

Chapter 28

Weird Prophecy, Weird Prophets
(2 Thessalonians 2:1–5)

Paul turns again to the theme of the Second Coming and refers to the time when all Christians will be gathered together by resurrection (1 Thessalonians 4:13–16) or by being *'caught up'* (1 Thessalonians 4:17) to meet Jesus and to be reunited with all believers. *'Now, brothers and sisters, with regard to the coming of our Lord Jesus Christ and our being assembling to him...'* (2:1). At the time of 1 Thessalonians there were people who dogmatically insisted that the Second Coming would come very soon indeed and that everyone would live to see the Second Coming of Jesus. At the time when 2 Thessalonians was written there were people who said that the Day of the Lord had come already! Apparently they were saying that Jesus had already secretly come (see Matthew 24:23 which predicted such people).

1. **There is a danger of odd teaching concerning Jesus' Second Coming**. People who are somewhat unstable or who like to declare new teachings, start thinking they know God's plan for the end of the world – although the same people often quieten down after a while, get married, find a good job and start planning for the future of their career! Paul writes to calm down those who were willing to believe that Jesus had already come. He says: *'we beg you not to be quickly shaken in your mind or disturbed, either by an inspired utterance or by a spoken word or by a letter said to be written by us, to the effect that the day of the Lord is present'* (2:2).

100

There was a lot of teaching like this going around. Sometimes someone would give a 'prophetic utterance' in one of the meetings in which an announcement would be made about the Second Coming. Sometimes the false teaching would be given in the form of a piece of teaching from one of the preachers. At some point a false letter had been received claiming to come from Paul, also giving strange teaching about the end of the world. (Some have said Paul did not write 2 Thessalonians. It would be strange if 2 Thessalonians were a fraudulent letter claiming to come from Paul – and yet complained about fraudulent letters claiming to come from Paul!)

We must not get too over-excited or fascinated by prophecy concerning the Second Coming. We must be ready for delay. For some people prophecy is very interesting, like reading a detective story, doing a jigsaw puzzle or a cross-word puzzle. Some people like trying to decipher things. They like trying to predict the future. But prophecy is not written so that we can predict what will happen and write about it before it happens. Remember that people who think they are experts in prophecy are nearly always proved wrong. People write books about what is going to happen. A few years later they are proved wrong. People do not predict what really is important. This has happened many times before. In the days of Napoleon, during the first and the second world wars, in the 1967 war when Israel invaded Sinai, during the rise of Russia since 1945, during the 'line-up of the planets' in 1981 (when the planets were more or less in a line) weird predictions were made. People have also often been fearful of modern inventions like machinery, television and other modern methods of communication, especially since the invention of the silicon chip, the credit card, and modern computer devices. There are always people who make odd prophecies. If you wait a few years, they are disproved – and then they make new ones!

It is not good to treat prophecy like this. Many of these 'prophetic experts' are really teaching that the Bible was irrelevant for most of the history of the church. But the Bible is a book that is relevant for the entire two thousand years of church history and more, maybe much more! But the 'prophetic experts' say is was written specially for us in this year when this and that prophecy is to be fulfilled. Such 'experts' are almost invariably proved wrong as time goes on. The major events of history are generally unexpected. Also, this style of interpretation is rather racist. It has a lot to say about USA, Europe, Russia, and western countries, but at the moment most Christians are in Africa, South America and certain parts of the Far East. This approach to prophecy takes us away from concern with evangelism, holiness, and the cross of Jesus, and gets us to focus on some exciting but weird interpretations of bits of Daniel or Revelation!

Prophecy is not written so that we can predict what will happen in detail. Rather, it tells us of the main facts and general trends of what will happen, so that we may cooperate with God's plan for reaching the world with the gospel of Jesus. Prophecy tells us about the Second Coming, the triumph of the gospel, the greatness of the opposition against the gospel, and it warns us that the Second Coming may be delayed.

2. **The appearing of the 'Man of Sin' precedes the Second Coming of Jesus** (2:3–5). The delay of the Second Coming gives a chance to the unsaved. It allows time for the progress of the gospel – and (as we learn here) allows evil to come to its full potential. *'See that no one deceives you by any means. That day will not arrive unless the rebellion comes first, and the Man of Lawlessness is revealed, the son of perdition (2:3), who opposes and exalts himself over against everything called god and against every object of worship, so that he takes his seat in the temple of God, proclaiming himself to be God (2:4). Do you not remember that I told you this while I was still with you?'* (2:5).

Although it is good to be always ready for Jesus to come – in one way or another – it is also true that certain major events have to happen before He will come. The idea that He might come 'at any second' is not quite right. *'That day will not arrive unless the rebellion comes first!'*

Chapter 29

The Man of Lawlessness
(2 Thessalonians 2:6–7)

There are both good days and tough days predicted for the future of the church. Among the good things predicted is the success of the gospel and the conversion of Israel. But there are tough times ahead as well. Paul says that the Second Coming of Jesus will not take place until after what he calls 'the rebellion'. 'Rebellion' or 'apostasy' or 'falling away' refers to a time when there is a large-scale abandonment of faith and godliness.

The law of Moses warned against these times (Exodus 20:3–4). So did Moses in his preaching (Deuteronomy 6:14; 11:16). Such times of 'falling away' have often occurred in the story of God's people. We may think of northern Israel during the days of king Ahab and queen Jezebel. Then there was a rebellion in the second century BC, predicted by Daniel chapter 8. Sometimes in these spiritual rebellions there is one particular man who rises up in opposition against God. The prophecy of Daniel predicted that there would be such a person in Israel. Daniel 8:5–8 undoubtedly refers to Alexander the Great. It was in the time of the Greek empire that there came 'a little horn which grew exceedingly'. Daniel 8:9–14 refers to Antiochus the Great who was the 'antichrist' of the Old Testament period.

In about 63 BC when the Roman emperor Pompei invaded Israel, many at that time also fell away from faith in the God of Israel.

Also about twelve years before Paul wrote 2 Thessalonians, there had been a mad emperor, Caligula, who had tried to set up his own statue in the temple in Jerusalem.

Jesus predicted that before the fall of Jerusalem there would be a similar period in which the love of many would grow cold. Then there would be an *'abomination of desolation'*, defiling the temple before it was destroyed.

Paul goes further than all of these events and predictions. Led by the Holy Spirit, Paul predicts that there will be a similar figure in the story of the church before the Second Coming of Jesus. It is not exactly identical to other passages and we must pay attention to Paul's words, rather than read them in the light of other events and predictions. As Paul puts it, there are two aspects to this coming opposition against the gospel. First there is a total disregard for God's will, a rebellion against God's authority (2:3a). *'That day will not arrive unless the rebellion comes first . . . '*.

Then there is a second aspect: *'. . . and the Man of Lawlessness is revealed'*. He predicts one particular person who will seek to overthrow God's will: he is a *'Man of Lawlessness'*. Like Judas Iscariot he is a *'son of perdition'*, a person doomed to failure, one who will inevitably come under God's judgement.

The *'Man of Lawlessness'* wants to oppose any kind of god (2:4a); he wants to be worshipped himself (2:4b) and will set himself up in God's temple. He *'takes his seat in the temple of God'*. This last phrase probably refers to the church; Paul's use of 'temple' often refers to the church (see Ephesians 2:21; 1 Corinthians 3:16, 17; 2 Corinthians 6:16).

Paul had given this teaching when he first visited Thessalonica (2:5). Now he wants to add some more. His main concern now is to speak of the delay and restraint of the *'Man of Lawlessness'*. People get excited about predictions of 'antichrist' just as they do about predictions of Jesus' coming. Paul wanted to calm the Thessalonians by letting them know Jesus was **not** coming until after the appearing of the Man of Lawlessness. He also wanted them to know that at present there is something restraining the Man of Lawlessness.

1. **The Restraint of the Man of Lawlessness**. At the time of Paul's writing lawlessness in the church was restrained. Paul says, *'And at this moment you know the thing that is restraining him, so that he might be revealed in his time* (2:6). *For the mystery of lawlessness is already operating; only the one who is restraining it will do so until he is removed'* (2:7).

The word 'mystery' means something that people can never know by themselves, that only God can reveal. God reveals to us that there is a permanent opposition to Jesus working all the time. It is as though Satan were simply waiting to introduce into the world greater rebellion against the gospel than ever, with one person that he will raise up to be his instrument.

But there is something or someone restraining this *'Man of Lawlessness'* from being raised up by Satan. The word translated *'restrain'* means 'hold' or 'hold on to' or 'control'. There is something or someone that is preventing Satan from raising up an arch-enemy of the gospel.

What is this *'restraint'*? (i) Is it the Roman empire or civil government? I do not find anything like this in Paul's teaching. (ii) Some have said the restrainer is the Holy Spirit, but I cannot see that the Holy Spirit will ever be 'removed'. (iii) Could the restrainer be an angelic power? Maybe.

(iv) The most likely 'restrainer' is Paul himself and the preaching of the gospel. This has parallels in Paul's teaching. Paul said that there was a danger of a *'falling away'* in Ephesus (see Acts 20:30), and we know that his prediction came true (see 2 Timothy 1:15). He could see lawlessness working and said that *'evil men will get worse and worse'* (2 Timothy 3:1–5, 13). Yet this development would get worse, he said, **after his departure** (Acts 20:29). He himself was having a restraining effect upon apostasy in Ephesus. We also know that the situation did get bad in Ephesus, and it was only the arrival of the apostle John that rescued the situation (see 1 John 2:19, written to Christians in the area of Ephesus). John calls this false teaching in the area of Ephesus 'antichrist' (1 John 2:18–27).

This all suggests that the 'thing that is restraining' is the gospel, and the 'one who is restraining' is the preacher of the gospel – supremely Paul himself. Only when the preaching of the gospel is removed does it become possible for *'the Man of Lawlessness'* to come.

Footnote

[1] Although I have put this interpretation my own way I am happy to have the support of O. Cullmann, 'Le caractère eschatologique...' *Revue d'histoire et de philosophie religieuses*, 16, 1936, pp. 210–245, and Munck, *Paul and the Salvation of Mankind* (SCM, 1954), pp. 36–42. However I think they should have emphasized that Paul thinks of himself as a representative of the work of a preacher. It is the Paul-type-of-person that restrains the Man of Lawlessness, not Paul as an individual.

Chapter 30

Lawlessness – Revealed and Destroyed

(2 Thessalonians 2:8–12)

2. **The Revealing of the Man of Lawlessness**. Paul's teaching is that at some stage in the gospel-age – the age we are in now between the First and Second Comings of Jesus – there will arise a great rebellion against God within the Christian church. 2 Thessalonians 2:1–12 is one of the notable parts of the Bible in its dealing with *'the Man of Lawlessness'* or *'antichrist'*. John uses the term *'antichrist'*[1]; Paul's term is *'Man of Lawlessness'*.

There is *'the thing that is restraining him, so that he might be revealed in his time'*. At the moment the *'mystery of lawlessness'* is being held back, Paul says: *'And then the lawless one will be revealed...'* (2:8). Before a miraculous 'revelation' of Jesus at the Second Coming, there is to be a wicked 'revelation' of the worst that Satan is able to do.

3. **The Ruination of the Man of Lawlessness**. Paul continues: *'...whom the Lord will slay[2] with the breath of His mouth and bring to an end by the appearance of His coming'* (2:8).

The Man of Lawlessness will be destroyed suddenly and easily. The *'breath of his mouth'* is simply a powerful word of command. The church lives by the word that proceeds from Jesus' mouth. The Man of Lawlessness does not last long. It does not seem that there is a long period between his appearing and his destruction. The breath of Jesus' mouth will soon destroy him.

4. **A reason for the Man of Lawlessness**. Paul now goes back to describe this Man of Lawlessness in fuller detail.

His power is satanic. Paul says *'This is the one whose coming is by the activity of Satan...'* (2:9). Just as Jesus' coming had miraculous activity behind it, so does the coming of the Man of Lawlessness. His rise to fame is satanic.

He is able to work miracles. Paul goes on to say the Man of Lawlessness comes *'with all power and signs and false wonders'* (2:9). That a man works signs and wonders does not prove much: so will the Man of Lawlessness!

He has power over the unsaved. Paul continued: *'... and with all the deception of wickedness for those who perish, because they did not receive the love of the truth so as to be saved'*. Within and around the church there will be those who are not truly saved. Such people are deceived by any miracle-working Man of Lawlessness who arises.

The coming of the Man of Lawlessness is a punishment. God may justly hand unbelieving people over to the power of their own unbelief. This is what will happen when the Man of Lawlessness comes. *'And for this reason God will send upon them a deluding influence so that they might believe what is false...'* (2:11). God can punish unbelief by leaving the unbeliever in the power of his own unbelief. He allows the Man of Lawlessness to succeed for a while, *'in order that they may be judged who did not believe the truth but took pleasure in wickedness'* (2:12).

5. **Some reflection upon the Man of Lawlessness**. We must give thought to how the Christian lives with predictions like these in the New Testament. We must not try to completely harmonize all of the predictions that the New Testament gives us, so as to make a time sequence of events.

There are predictions of success for the gospel. There are predictions of lawlessness. How do these fit together? Is the apostasy after the conversion of Israel? Is there to be a great desertion of the Christian faith and then a powerful *'breath of his mouth'* that brings revival and restoration for the church – and then the Man of Lawlessness is utterly destroyed? That is, could he be destroyed in two stages? This is what was believed in the seventeenth century. Or is it that there will be a glorious age for the church and then a great apostasy?

I do not think we are meant to know the answer to these questions. Remember that when Jesus came the first time there were prophecies of suffering and prophecies of glory for the Messiah. Believers did not know how to fit those prophecies together and when Jesus came the first time no one had the right interpretation!

The right way to live with biblical prophecy is not to try to write the history books before the events happen, but to keep the different prophecies in mind as we proceed with the work of the Lord. We expect the glorious success of the gospel. We expect Israel to be saved and the church to be brought to glorious maturity (as Ephesians 4:11–16 promises). We also know that all the time the mystery of lawlessness is working against Jesus and that at one stage he will be allowed a measure of success – for a little while. We know that his final destruction will come at the Second Coming, which implies that the Man of Lawlessness will not be finally and totally put down until Jesus comes.

Yet Paul carried on with his work of evangelising Europe, restraining the Man of Lawlessness by the powerful preaching of Jesus' word. It will be the power of Jesus' word also that destroys the Man of Lawlessness when he comes. Perhaps he will be destroyed partly by a remnant preaching God's word, and partly by Jesus' coming. It is a basic principle of prophetic interpretation: the final interpretation is the event itself!

One day we shall know. Meanwhile we are encouraged; the church will triumph, righteousness will conquer, Jesus will come. Yet we are also warned; a mystery of lawlessness is at work and always will be. Only preaching the gospel holds it down. Only Jesus' coming is its final abolition.

Footnotes

[1] See M.A. Eaton, *1, 2, 3 John: Focus on the Bible* (Christian Focus, 1996), chapters 8–9, for expositions of John's teaching concerning Antichrist.

[2] The word is *analei*, 'kill'. The KJV translation 'consume' depends on an inferior text using a different Greek verb, *analisko*.

Chapter 31

The Security of God's People

(2 Thessalonians 2:13–17)

Several events are expected before the Second Coming. The
Bible invites us to be reaching all nations and continue to do
so even to the end of the age (Matthew 28:18–20). The kingdom of God has to work like leaven. Israel has to be saved
(Romans 11:25–26). Perilous times will come (2 Timothy
3:1–5). Jesus warned people not to think the kingdom of
God should immediately appear (Luke 19:11–27). The bridegroom will delay (Matthew 25:5). Only *after a long time*
does the Master come to settle accounts (Matthew 25:19).

We are certainly to be eager for the Second Coming of
Jesus (see Matthew 16:26, 27; Luke 12:8, 35–37; 1 Corinthians 3:13; Philippians 3:20; Colossians 3:4, 5; 2 Timothy
4:8; James 5:7; 1 Peter 1:13; 4:12, 13; 2 Peter 3:9, 10; 1 John
2:28; 3:2, 3; Jude 14, 15; Revelation 1:7; 2:25). Eagerly looking for the Second Coming of Jesus is a distinctive mark of
the Christian. The Thessalonians were waiting for God's Son
to come from heaven (1 Thessalonians 1:9, 10). So were the
Corinthians (1 Corinthians 1:7, 8).

Yet we must remember that **the Second Coming can be
experienced as a foretaste**. The *Day of the Lord* may be
experienced at any moment. There come times in the story of
the world when God 'comes' and it looks as if it is the end of
the world – and yet history goes on. It turns out that 'the
end' was only a foretaste, only a kind of preview of the end
of the world. In this sense we may know that Jesus' 'coming'

might be experienced **by way of foretaste** even before the very final Second Coming itself. In the Old Testament great crises were regarded as *'the day of the Lord'*. They were previews of the end of the world. *'The end is coming on the four corners of the land'*, said Ezekiel (7:2). *'The end has come'* (Ezekiel 7:6)! *'The day has arrived'* (Ezekiel 7:12)! Yet history went on. 'The end' that Ezekiel spoke of was a preview of the end. It was the end brought forward. Similarly the fall of Jerusalem was a kind of preview of the Second Coming of Jesus (as Matthew 24 makes clear).

The Second Coming may well be delayed; yet it may be experienced at any moment! We watch moment by moment for Jesus' coming – even if only by preview and foretaste. We never know when Jesus might not step into world history and **our** world may end, though the world as a whole continues.

Meanwhile there is work to be done and 'the Man of Lawlessness' is already at work. Yet Paul says the Christian need not fear. Over against the threat of the Man of Lawlessness, God's people stand secure. They are secure because of what has happened to them, because of their salvation.

1. **They are secure because God has chosen them**. God's plan cannot be overthrown. Paul says: *'But we should always give thanks to God for you, brothers and sisters, beloved by the Lord, because God has chosen you from the beginning for salvation through sanctification by the Spirit and faith in the truth'* (2:13).

A great plan has been at work. God chose them for salvation. The Holy Spirit worked in their lives and *'set them apart'*. *'Sanctification'* in this verse does not have its meaning of growth in godliness. It refers to something that happens when God first works in our lives to bring us to salvation. God changes our nature, enables us to believe in Jesus, and draws us powerfully to His Son.

If we see that our salvation is part of a great plan of God, we shall feel secure. We shall know that we are safe because we know that God is not intending to give up on His plan to have us and keep us. Even the terrors of the Man of Lawlessness will not shake us. God's people are secure.

2. **They are secure because God has plans to bring them to glory**. If God has started with them, He will go on working in them to the end. Paul says: *'And it was for this salvation that He called you through our gospel, that you may gain the glory of our Lord Jesus Christ'* (2:14). God has given them a secure position. From that secure position they are to serve God so as to be rewarded by God in the final day when Jesus comes. God has a purpose at work in them. Their position is safe but the purpose needs to be worked out. They must *'work out their salvation'* because God is at work in them to bring about His purposes (see Philippians 2:12–13).

So then there are certain things they must do.

1. **They must stand firm**. If God has made them safe, they must act that way. *'So then, brothers, stand firm...'*.

2. **They must hold to the Word of God**. Paul says they must stand firm *'and hold to the traditions which you were taught, whether by spoken word or by letter from us'* (2:15). They must hold on to the message of the gospel, in all of its aspects. They must believe the teaching, experience the power, live out the life of the gospel of Jesus. The message has come to them in various forms. Paul has given them oral teaching. He has sent them an inspired letter and now this second letter is another inspired writing for them to study and hold fast.

3. **They must know that he will continue in faithful praying for them**. Paul brings this part of his letter to a close by praying for them, then and there, in writing. *'Now may our Lord Jesus Christ Himself and God our Father, who has loved us and given us eternal comfort and good hope by grace...'* (2:16). Paul's prayer begins by looking at what God has already done. Then it goes on to the actual request: *'...comfort and strengthen your hearts in every work and word'* (2:16). This is the way Paul will be praying for them. We need steady assurance; we need strong hearts; we need to act and to speak. Paul's prayers are good hints as to how we should pray also.

Chapter 32

Paul's Confidence

(2 Thessalonians 3:1–5)

1. **Paul's confidence in prayer**. We have seen a number of references to prayer in these letters (see 1:2–3; 3:10, 3:9–13; 5:17, 23–24, 25). Now again (see 1 Thessalonians 5:25) Paul asks for prayer. It is obvious that Paul is confident in the power of prayer. These Thessalonians are young Christians. We might think Paul will only say 'I am praying for you', but he wants their prayers also. *'As for the rest of what I want to say – brothers and sisters, pray for us...'*

How much we pray depends a lot on how confident we are that prayer will be answered. Paul obviously felt the need of praying himself. He knew his converts would decline if he did not pray. He knew that he himself would decline if people did not pray for him.

There were two things he specially wanted prayer for. He wanted them to pray *'that the word of the Lord may make speedy progress and be honoured, just as it was with you'* (3:1). Paul did not want them pray about money or comforts or for an easy life. His supreme concern was for the message of the gospel. And he wanted prayer that he would be protected as he persevered with this work: *'and that we may be delivered from perverse and evil men, for not all people have faith'* (3:2). There were many dangers for Paul. Jewish people who did not believe Jesus was the Messiah would oppose him at every step. Pagan people whose money-making corrupt ways and hatred of righteousness were challenged by the gospel, hated

Paul's preaching. He was in 'danger from rivers, danger from robbers, danger from his own people, danger ... everywhere (see 2 Corinthians 11:26)!

The passing phrase, *'not all people have faith'*, is an important one. Faith is not a natural virtue. We cannot say 'Everyone has faith! Switch your faith on!' – as some like to do. We shall never win everyone, and it is a miracle from above every time we win anyone.

2. **Paul's confidence in God's faithfulness**. There were many dangers for Paul yet he says: *'However the Lord is faithful, and he will confirm you and will guard you from the evil one'* (3:3). Paul is confident in God's faithfulness. Amidst great opposition and fearful circumstances, Paul is willing to stand still and see the deliverances of God. Though he may at times be weak, God is never weak. Though he may let God down, God will never let him down. Though we are faithless, He abides faithful.

He is confident that because of God's faithfulness, his converts will be able to stand. God will support their faith and will give them protection against Satan.

3. **Paul's confidence in his converts**. It is amazing how much Paul maintained confidence in God and yet took much responsibility himself. He left his new converts to grow somewhat independently of him. He cared for them, but he cared for them in a way that let them stand on their own feet. *'And we are confident in the Lord about you'*, he says, *'that you are doing the things we are commanding you, and that you will continue to do so'* (3:4). Although he is some distance away from them he feels sure that God is able to keep them in the ways of obedience to God's word which he has given them. Paul believes that from the very first days, his converts are able to be equipped with spiritual authority. His churches grew rapidly because he trusted God to be at work in them. He did not establish 'mission-posts'. He established churches and he let them have their own character from day one. He never corrupted them by making them financially dependent on him. It took a lot of faith in God and a lot of prayer!

So he prays. *'And may the Lord direct your hearts into the love of God and to the perseverance of Christ'* (3:5). The great thing he is concerned about is Christian character and among the very first items he has on his mind are their love for each other and their perseverance amidst the persecution and opposition at Thessalonica.

For us too, the greatest goals and aims of our life must focus on faith, love and hope: the three highpoints of Christian character. Nothing is of any value without them. Paul has said much about faith. He hopes it will work itself out in Christian love and steadfastness.

Love makes them work for God (1 Thessalonians 1:3). He knows that they are a people of love already (1 Thessalonians 3:6) and he has asked them to continue in love for each other (1 Thessalonians 3:12). It will be a protection to them, a breastplate (1 Thessalonians 5:8). He particularly hopes they will show love to the leaders of the church (1 Thessalonians 5:13). In writing this second letter to them he has expressed his gratitude for their continued love among themselves (2 Thessalonians 1:3). Now he gives himself again to praying about this very matter; he asks that the Lord Jesus Christ may direct them more and more into the pathways of love. It implies that they will be in fellowship and contact with the Lord Jesus Christ and that He will guide them and direct them. Underlying is the knowledge that they have a *'love of the truth'* – a phrase he has already used (2 Thessalonians 2:10). Love of the gospel is the starting point of love for people.

He also prays that they will be a people of perseverance. There are many forces working against them at Thessalonica. It will take perseverance if they are to survive, as the apostle is sure they will. He has spoken to them already of their persistence, the *'endurance that comes from your expectation concerning our Lord Jesus'* (1 Thessalonians 1:3), and of how he boasted about their steadfastness (2 Thessalonians 1:4). Now he makes it a matter of continued prayer; he asks that they might be helped by Jesus into staying strong amidst the dark and dangerous circumstances in Thessalonica, until it is transformed by their witness and their message to the world around them.

Chapter 33

Toil or Trouble?

(2 Thessalonians 3:6–10)

There were people in Thessalonica who had claimed to
be Christians and had responded to the preaching of the
gospel, yet were living in an undisciplined way. They were
irresponsible people who were careless about doing any
work.

1. **Paul teaches that idleness is contrary to the apostolic
tradition**. The church of Jesus Christ has a tradition. It has a
store of teachings that were 'handed down' from Jesus
through the first generation of apostles to the church. Paul
writes: *'Now, brothers and sisters, we command you in the
name of the Lord Jesus Christ to disassociate yourself from
any brother or sister who is living in idleness, and not according
to the tradition which you received from us'* (3:6).

'Tradition' does not refer to accumulating customs and
doctrines that churches pick up as the years go by. The reference is not to additions to the Bible or denominational rules
and regulations that become 'traditional'. Paul certainly
would not approve of new doctrines that creep into the
church and become 'traditional' – such as the 'tradition' that
says Mary was free from sin.

The basic gospel message was a matter of teaching being
passed on. The tradition began with Jesus. The Thessalonians
'received' the apostolic preaching of Paul (1 Thessalonians 2:13). Jesus gave it to Paul on the Damascus Road, and
Paul passed it on.

Also there were sayings of Jesus that were passed on in this way. 1 Corinthians 7:10–11; 9:14 and 1 Timothy 5:18 are examples.

The teaching about the Lord's Supper was 'passed on' as a matter of tradition (see 1 Corinthians 11:23).

There were also traditions coming from Jesus and the apostle about life-style and good living, as we can see from 1 Corinthians 11:2. 2 Thessalonians 3:6 is similar. The apostles taught the Thessalonians that it was necessary to be active in seeking to earn an honest livelihood. It was part of apostolic teaching that was 'handed down' to new Christians; Christians should find some form of work. Even if 'unemployed' because of high levels of unemployment in a nation, there is much that God will give Christians to do. People who do little work but spend their time raising excitement about the end of the world, are departing from the tradition passed down by Jesus and His apostle, Paul. It is not a matter of new doctrines or customs being added by 'tradition'. But we are to follow the teachings that come from Jesus and the first apostles, which they handed down to us. The traditions were not only oral; they could be handed down in writing as well (see 2 Thessalonians 2:15).

2. **Paul teaches that idleness is contrary to his own example**. Paul has given them a good example. He was not undisciplined: *'For you yourselves know you ought to imitate us, because we did not live in idleness among you...'* (3:7). Christian living has to be taught by example as well as by word. Paul deliberately gave the Thessalonians an example, when he earned himself some money by getting some paid employment in Thessalonica. He pointed to himself as a model of how to be a Christian. It was not that he was utterly perfect, but he could say *'Remember me in everything'* (1 Corinthians 11:2). *'Continue doing the things that you have learned and received and heard and seen in me...'* (Philippians 4:9).

Paul was especially careful about money: *'and we did not eat anyone's bread without paying for it, but with toil and hardship we worked night and day, so that we should not burden any of you'* (3:8).

Christian workers may well have to be willing to be financially self-sufficient. Jesus was a carpenter. Paul could make tents. Many ministers have had to do some school-teaching or work in an office. In many parts of the world pastors do a little carpentry or some farming.

3. **Paul teaches that a preacher may well have to give an example of diligence in ordinary work**. It is not wrong to receive support but sometimes we have to set a good example by not being a burden to the people to whom we minister. *'It is not that we have no rights in this matter, but we did what we did to offer ourselves as an example for you to imitate'* (3:9). Paul sometimes deliberately avoided being supported so that he could free to be a good example in his approach to money. It seems that this was a special problem in Thessalonica. Some were lazy. They would spread gossip and foolish rumours about antichrist or about Jesus' coming. They wanted to be supported by other Christians. Paul deliberately showed them another way.

4. **Paul teaches that lazy people should receive no support**. They should be rebuked by the church deliberately disassociating itself from such people. The outsider must not be allowed to get a false impression. The idlers should get no support. *'For when we were with you we gave you this command, "If a person does not want to work, let him not eat"'* (3:10). Paul has a lot of sympathy for people who are in need (as 2 Corinthians chapters 8 and 9, Romans 15:26–29, Galatians 2:10, make clear) but he deals severely with Christians who love excitement but have no love of work.

The Christian 'work-ethic' is visible here. The Bible allows plenty of scope for rest. The Mosaic law demanded that 14% of the week should be restful (in the keeping of the Sabbath). Yet the leading of the Spirit will not tolerate easygoing attitudes to work, and will not guide us into indolence. Paul knows what is the leading of the Spirit. Work was part of paradise (Genesis 2:15). Work is not necessarily paid employment. There are other ways in which we can be active for God and make a contribution to this world. Certainly laziness is not to be supported by the church. *'If a person does not want to work, let him not eat'.*

Chapter 34

A Pastor's Word of Authority
(2 Thessalonians 3:11–15)

Paul is dealing with the brothers and sisters *'who are living in idleness'* (3:6). He has urged the church to disassociate itself from such people (3:6–10). Now he addresses the careless Christians directly.

1. **Paul has the courage to rebuke these idle people directly**. The Christian gospel is not just a theory, not just a doctrine. Paul is not giving these Thessalonian Christians popular lectures in doctrine. He is not simply saying things that are interesting. He is concerned with life and behaviour and spirituality. He says: *'For we hear that some of you are living in idleness, not doing any work but being meddlesome'* (3:11). It is a very bold statement, very forthright. However Paul is not being rude. He does not mention any names. He is not wanting to be insulting, but the Christian teaching has to get to grips with our actual living. So the preacher or pastor has to have the courage to apply the biblical teaching. We have to apply it to ourselves first; it can be very painful to do so! Then we have to apply the Scriptures and take steps to see that the word of God is being practically obeyed. So he is blunt. *'Some of you are living in idleness'*, he says. *'You are being meddlesome'*. Some of the Thessalonians were running around stirring up excitement about the Day of the Lord, and telling others what to do – but doing no practical work and depending on the charity of others to eat! Paul is a

faithful pastor. He rebukes them by impressing upon them what he knows is God's will for them.

2. **He puts to them the positive challenge concerning the way they should live**. It is not enough simply to rebuke. The positive challenge must be presented also. *'Now such people we command and exhort in the Lord Jesus Christ, that by doing some work in calmness they may earn their own living'* (3:12). Paul is not being arrogant or dictatorial. He speaks *'in the Lord Jesus Christ'*. A pastor or preacher may sometimes speak authoritatively and commandingly. It is not that he is being dictatorial. It does not necessarily mean that he has a domineering attitude or a conceited view of himself. Paul speaks *'in the Lord Jesus Christ'*.

So he is firm and emphatic. These idlers must learn to start working and earning their own living. They must stop getting excited about themselves and stop using the doctrine of the Second Coming to draw attention to themselves. They must settle down and get on with living the Christian life.

3. **He has a word of encouragement to the obedient Christians**. He has already commended the church (3:4–5). Many of the Christians have been faithful and conscientious, unlike these idlers who were getting over-excited about the Second Coming. Paul has a word for them. *'And you, brothers and sisters, do not become weary in well-doing'* (3:13). The Christians generally were getting somewhat depressed and fatigued by these many troubles. The people of Thessalonica had been oppressing them. The excited idlers had been troubling them with excesses concerning the Second Coming of Jesus. They had been finding these brothers and sisters very meddlesome. Paul says, go on living a faithful life. Do not become weary in well-doing. It is *'well-doing'*! The way you have been living has been good, says Paul. Don't get weary. Remember you are serving Jesus and go on.

4. **The idlers must be severely rebuked if they will not heed these apostolic commands**. They have publicly refused to amend their ways and are defying Paul's teaching and his example. The matter is a serious one. *'If anyone does not obey our instruction through this letter, note that person, and do not associate with him, in order to bring him to be ashamed'* (3:14).

The Christians must express their disapproval of the ways of the idlers. The whole congregation is responsible and must take action. Yet the discipline must be exercised in a loving way. Paul says: *'Yet do not regard that person as an enemy, but reprimand that one as a brother or sister'* (3:15). The disorderly person must be disciplined (3:14) yet treated with love (3:15). The hope is that the inconsistent Christians will feel ashamed of what they have been doing and will mend their ways.

Paul speaks very authoritatively. He is a first-generation apostle, and an eye-witness of the resurrection of Jesus from the dead. He is one of the ones upon whom the church is being built in its very earliest days. Can anyone speak with authority like this today? Only if they do so via the New Testament. Modern church leaders can speak with authority only via the teaching of the first generation of apostles. Christians have different opinions over whether there can be 'apostles' today, but one thing is sure. No one is precisely an eye-witness of the resurrection as the apostle Paul was. No one can lay down any new doctrines of the faith, as Peter and Paul and the other first apostles could do. Any authority we have is via the authority they had. We have no authority to contradict their authority.

The Christian church leader has a model in Paul in these lines. He presents the teaching but he does not leave it simply as 'teaching'. He presses upon Christians the need to work out what he says in the way in which they live. He insists on the work being done. If any do not apply what he teaches to their lives, he rebukes them, lovingly. If they will not heed his rebukes he demands that the church call them to account. Yet at the same time he takes steps to make sure that no one is discouraged. Those who are rebuked must be treated as brothers and sisters, not as enemies. Those who need no rebuke are encouraged to continue and not get weary. Paul is a pattern of a balanced and practical Christian ministry.

Chapter 35

Jesus Christ Our Lord

(2 Thessalonians 3:16–18)

Paul comes to the end of his second letter to the Thessalonians. He prays for them (3:16), signs his letter as a mark of genuineness (3:17), and says his final prayer for the grace of God to be at work in their lives (3:18).

1. **He prays for their peace**. There was surely a special need for such a prayer in the church. The Christians were facing opposition. Busybodies were spreading excited teaching that was not helping anyone. Now the apostle has spoken words of rebuke about them, and has demanded they be reprimanded by the congregation if they will not repent. The congregation is in special need of God's peace and so Paul makes it a matter of prayer. *'Now may the Lord of peace himself give you peace at all times and in every way. The Lord be with you all'* (3:16).

What is this peace? It certainly is not the peace of an easy life. Jesus did not come to bring that sort of peace. 'Peace' is a sense of reconciliation with God plus the assurance of His care. It begins by our knowing that God is our Father and our friend. We are reconciled to Him and so are at peace with Him. But more than that, peace is the conviction that God is able to handle all disputes, all troubles, all busybodies, all persecutors.

Jesus wants to give them such peace. He Himself is the Lord of peace. It is something that ought to be constantly enjoyed by the Christian and this is the way Paul prays. It should be uninterrupted. Paul prays for the special Christian peace to be among his friends *'at all times and in every way'*. It is something that should not be lost and we must take special steps to pray for its restoration if we lose it. Jesus Himself will draw near to His people and give them His assurance that all is well with them.

2. **He checks that the people will know what is genuinely his teaching**. There were some forged documents around claiming to come from Paul. Paul has a way of dealing with it. He signs his letters in a special way. If his friends get any letter not signed in precisely the way he ends them – then the letter is not genuine.

Paul used an *amanuensis* – a secretary. He dictated his letters and his assistant wrote them for him. But towards the end of the letter Paul takes the pen into his own hands and adds something with a very special style. *'I, Paul, write this greeting with my own hand, which is a sign. In every letter I write this way'* (3:17).

It might seem surprising that anyone should take the trouble to pretend to be Paul and spread around false teaching pretending that it is Paul's teaching, but the dishonesty of false teachers is great. Deceit deadens the conscience and false teachers will be quite untruthful in doing anything to get their teaching heeded.

Nowadays forged letters from Paul are not a problem but there are still modern ways in which people avoid Paul's teaching. It may be simply neglected. People give teaching claiming to be 'the Word of God' yet perhaps make no real reference to the Scriptures. Or they 'use' them selectively twisting the Scriptures and pulling texts out of context to give weight to doctrines that they never got from the Scriptures at all!

Paul's teaching has a certain amount of credibility. People want to get the name of Paul on their side! In the first century they forged letters. Today many will make fraudulent claims to be presenting scriptural teaching when perhaps they have a very weak grasp of the Scriptures.

3. **The ultimate need is for God's grace to be at work in our lives**. Life is complicated! What a mass of perplexities and

hindrances to godliness Paul has had to handle. His final prayer should come as no surprise to us. *'The grace of our Lord Jesus Christ be with all of you'* (3:18).

The one thing every Christian needs is God's grace, God's active help working in our lives, God's undeserved favour sustaining us. At times the battle of the Christian life might seem to be too great, but God's grace is sufficient for every situation. God never allows us to get into any circumstance where His grace is inadequate.

It is the grace *'of our Lord Jesus Christ'* that is needed. Jesus is the source. Jesus is the channel. It originates in what He did for us on the cross. It came into our lives when He came into our lives. It flows day by day into our experience as we lean on the actual presence of Jesus with us. It comes as we look for it, as we pray for it, as Paul is praying in these last words.

Paul sometimes likes to use the full expression when he refers to Jesus: *'our Lord Jesus Christ'*. Jesus! The one who was born as a real human being at Bethlehem, who knows how to sympathize with me as a fellow human being. Christ! The one anointed with the power of the Holy Spirit and who is able to rule over my every circumstance and situation. The Lord! The one who is as much divine as the Father, the Creator, the Sustainer of the universe, the Conqueror of Satan.

Above all: 'our' Lord. The one to whom we have given our life, the one who has promised never to leave us or forsake us, the one from whose hands we cannot be taken, the one from whom we can never be separated. Life is complicated; it is sin and Satan that make it so. But with *'our Lord Jesus Christ'* and the grace that He gives, we can overcome anything, and live for His praise.

More Advanced Reading

For further study I recommend the following works.

For general interpretation, most helpful are: F.F. Bruce, *1 & 2 Thessalonians* (Word 1982), L. Morris, *The First and Second Epistles to the Thessalonians* (Eerdmans, 1959), P. Ellingworth and E.A. Nida, *A Translator's Handbook on Paul's Letters to the Thessalonians* (UBS, 1976).

B. Rigaux, *Les Epitres Aux Thessaloniciens* (Gabalda, 1956) is excellent for those who read French.

Other commentaries by Barclay, Best, Eadie, Ellicott, Findlay, Frame, Lenski, Milligan, Moffatt, Moore, Olshausen, Plummer, Walwoord, Wanamaker, and others, are less useful or not needed in addition to the larger commentaries. Only the most thorough students need consult them.

For theological exposition, works by W. Hendriksen, *I and II Thessalonians* (Baker, 1955) and J.R.W. Stott, *The Message of Thessalonians* (IVP, 1991) are valuable. Also useful are J. Calvin, *1 and 2 Thessalonians* (1550, various translations), J. Denney, *The Epistles to the Thessalonians* (1892; available in libraries or second-hand), Fergusson and Dickson, *Galatians, Ephesians, Philippians, Colossians, Thessalonians, and Hebrews* (Banner of Truth, reprinted 1978), D.E. Hiebert, *The Thessalonian Epistles* (Moody, 1971), C.F. Hogg and W.E. Vine, *The Epistles to the Thessalonians* (Pickering & Inglis, 1914).

C.H. Giblin's work on 2 Thessalonians, chapter 2, *Threat to Faith* is worth reading. Thomas Manton preached on

2 Thessalonians 1 and 2, and those sermons are available in the *Complete Works of Thomas Manton*, volumes 3 and 20.

Also some works on the Second Coming are useful in connection with the teaching concerning the Second Coming: M.J. Erickson's *Contemporary Options in Eschatology* (Baker, 1977), and R.H. Gundry's *The Church and The Tribulation* (Zondervan, 1973).